FEARLESS LOVE

FEARLESS LOVE

Astounding stories of God's intervention in Islamic Africa

James Andrews

Authentic

British Library Cataloguing in Publication Data

A catalogue record for this book is available from the
British Library

ISBN: 978-1-85078-982-6

Cover design by Phil Houghton
Printed and bound by CPI Group (UK) Ltd, Croydon, CR0 4YY

Hereby perceive we the love of God, because he laid down his life for us: and we ought to lay down our lives for the brethren.
The Apostle John
(1 John 3:16, KJV)

'I am not against Muslims although I am against Islam as a false religion. I don't want to disgrace Muslims but to expose Islam. My ultimate intention is to glorify God and to save people, especially Muslims. Muslims are victims.'
Zakaria Botros
(http://www.diaryof1.com/2009/01/25/zakaria-botros-unafraid-to-defy-islam/
accessed 1 July 2011)

'Faith brings the man to God, love brings him to men.'
Martin Luther
('The Day of the Holy Innocents', *The Complete Sermons of Martin Luther*,
Grand Rapids, MI: Baker Books, 2000 Vol. 7, p.225–56)

Dedicated with thanks to God and to the team:
the founding leaders, staff, students and
supporters of the outreach.

No part of this work is fiction. All names have
been changed to protect the identity of those
involved, and location names have been
withheld. James Andrews is a pseudonym.

CONTENTS

Author Note

In the book we describe some aspects of the impact *Sharia* law is having in areas where we serve the gospel of Jesus Christ. We are not experts on world religions, and the book's main endeavour is to describe the love of God working in people's lives in the midst of opposition to the gospel message. Many of the Muslim people we have met and work with would ordinarily be loving people, if not forced into a wrong lifestyle by the dictates of *Sharia* and those who promote it. Those who have not received Jesus' love are lost in sin, and we all need his redeeming power to set us free, no matter our cultural or religious background.

Prologue

A team of friends and leaders have relocated to the north of a large, well-populated nation, in the vicinity of the huge Islamic harvest field in the African Sahel, just south of the Sahara desert. An outreach has been established that includes a rapidly expanding group of affiliated churches, an accredited Bible college, new mission stations in unreached areas, a primary school, vocational training and gospel outreach through pastors' conferences, evangelism, printed literature, weekly television and radio broadcasts. The outreach extends to nations around the Sahara and north into Egypt and the Middle East. This book tells the story of their mission to reach people with the gospel in the midst of violent Islamic *jihad*.

Unless otherwise stated, references in this book to a 'college' refer to the Bible college established by this outreach.

Introduction

To the casual observer, there was nothing unusual about the little family: the small boy strapped securely onto his mother's back with a length of once-bright printed cloth, her husband standing protectively beside them. Just another village family waiting for a taxi, travelling perhaps to visit relatives in the city.

Dawn was breaking over the pot-holed parking lot where other small groups waited to cram into the third- or fourth-hand Japanese cars that provide one of Africa's cheapest forms of public transport. The other member of their party, a man who had been negotiating with the driver of a taxi that was almost full, beckoned the family across. They squeezed themselves in, and the taxi pulled away. Nothing remarkable. And if an observer had noticed the looks of relief on all their faces; well, it's understandable to be relieved at nearing the end of a long journey.

No one could possibly have guessed how long and dangerous this particular family's journey had been. And as for nearing the end – it had only just begun. Cut off from relatives and friends, exiled from their home, they had embarked on a lifelong journey that would certainly mean persecution, and perhaps even death.

In the taxi, John smiled at the family. Though he'd chatted casually with the other passengers to make sure none were likely to recognize them, it was still not safe to speak freely. The couple were some of the first Christian converts at a new mission station far from the Bible college where John worked. However, their remote village was entirely Muslim, and had reacted with violence to the family's refusal to give up their new-found faith and return to Islam. They had received death threats, and their own parents, furious that their children had brought shame on them, had offered a reward for their capture. The family fled to a friend's house in a nearby town, where they borrowed some clothes to make them less recognizable. In the middle of the night, they were smuggled out to the home of another friend in a different city. They were now on their way to a refuge house connected to the Bible college, and although they were far from their village, they were not yet safe. If they were discovered, John knew, they would surely be killed.

By early evening, the taxi was speeding towards the crowded city, and the Bible college. John was relieved that they would make the 6 p.m. curfew – if they had been too late, the car and its passengers would have been held at one of the military checkpoints on the outskirts until morning, and he was anxious to get the family to a safe house as soon as possible.

Dry, dusty winds from the Sahara in the north were giving way to evening rains as the wet season pushed up from the southern tropics. The city was jammed with traffic negotiating pot-holes, and stallholders in the street markets packing up for the day. A nearby mosque sounded the call to evening prayer. The small boy stared out of the window, his eyes wide. With almost a million inhabitants, the city's sheer size would be overwhelming after life in a small village.

Amidst the hustle and bustle, there was a strong undercurrent of anxiety. Armoured vehicles and tanks patrolled the streets. There were heavily armed soldiers at the frequent checkpoints, carefully scrutinizing the passengers and prodding goods with the barrels of their machine-guns before each vehicle was allowed to pass. Two weeks earlier there had been a sudden attack against Christians. Churches at different points in the city had been ambushed during their Sunday morning worship, and in the days that followed hundreds of people were killed. A student from the Bible college had escaped from his church as the building was set ablaze, but others had been struck down trying to reach safety.

John glanced back at the family. They had escaped one danger only to face another; yet, as they laughed and joked in the crowded taxi, the power, presence and love of God were much more apparent than fear. Despite all they had lost, they did not regret their decision to hold to their new faith.

At long last the taxi stopped in a large compound. This was home to the Bible college, as well as many small apartment buildings. John helped the family out, and ushered them towards his flat, where his wife, Patience – relief showing on her face – waited to greet him. John's wife and two small daughters had been moved to a safer location during the worst of the violence, but were now back home. The children flung themselves joyfully at their father. The new family would stay with them that night, and in the morning John would take them to the college and their new home.

The compound still bore the marks of the attacks a fortnight ago, and most of the occupants of the flats had fled, leaving the college staff to protect the housing estate. One of the buildings had been burnt to the ground, and the security fence surrounding the estate destroyed. The majority of the buildings outside the perimeter wall were now burnt-out shells. The whole district resembled a war zone: it neither looked nor felt very safe, but that night no further violence disturbed the curfew.

The next morning, everyone was up early, and in good spirits. John's 4-year-old daughter helped her mother sweep the rooms clean with a straw hand-broom, singing Christian choruses as she swept. Then Patience cooked breakfast for everyone – scrambled eggs, tomato and chilli with bread, and Lipton tea – with her youngest child tied on her back to keep her out of mischief.

It was time to take the family to see the college they had heard so much about. Passing small vegetable plots between the compound flats, John led them towards a large two-storey building, its freshly painted exterior setting it apart from the rest. At the office near the entrance, he introduced them to Jacob, the college dean, who offered a traditional greeting in Hausa, the trade language of the area: *'Ina kwana?'* ('How did you sleep?'). *'Lafi ya'*, ('fine') they responded, politely.

By now, classes were under way, and the family was ushered into a room full of students listening intently to a study on the cross of Christ. Jesus said, 'take up [your] cross, and follow me' (Matt. 16:24, KJV) and 'If they did this to me, they will also do it to you' (see John 15:20). The family knew the truth of this, first-hand. To those assembled, the family's circumstances were also familiar: many of the students had experienced the same rejection, exile and loss of relatives and property, and their lives were also at risk because of their new-found faith.

Christians are sometimes accused of irresponsibly causing divisions within communities and families by preaching the gospel, and there are those who argue that it would have been better to leave the people in blissful ignorance. Yet when the students heard of freedom from guilt and sin, of new life in the love of God, they did not choose oppression but gladly chose faith, with all they knew they would suffer because of it. To fail to reach others with the gospel is to defy the commission of Jesus to the church. Jesus made it clear: 'He who is not with me is against me, and he who does not gather with me, scatters' (Luke 11:23, NIV).

Many hours' drive from the city, in villages with only a worn footpath for access, mission centres like the one where the family heard the gospel are already reaping the rich harvest of people sincerely desiring truth. Bible college graduates from remote regions return to their home area, sharing the gospel from compound to mud-brick houses. Ethnic Fulani graduates trek between cattle-herding camps to share the gospel with the nomadic Fulani. No non-Fulani has such access to this elitist group of people, nor would dare to venture there. But in every place, people are hungry to know the gospel.

Many converts are forced to flee, just like Paul in the book of Acts. This is a common consequence of having mission stations reaching both Muslims and pagans. Some, like this particular family, are taken to a refuge house, but others move into the college compound to stay with staff and students. After they are nurtured and have grown in their faith, many are able to return to their home area, where the Lord uses them to spread the gospel: like Samson's foxes with their tails set on fire (see Judg. 15:3–5), they are sent into the harvest fields. To preach faithfully is to be prepared to care for the new believers, whatever that might cost. The college could not abandon this family in their time of need. For the gospel to grow in Islamic regions, those who come to Jesus must be supported.

The students encouraged the family, and gave them spare clothing and other things that they would need before John took them to the other side of the city to their refuge house. Amos, the converted Muslim who ran the refuge house, had arranged to meet them at his office unit in the market-place, where he sold sacks of rice. It was about a kilometre away from the refuge house – he had to be sure that the new refugees were genuine before he took them to his home.

Many people are under sentence of death from *Sharia* law courts, for the crime of converting from Islam to Christianity, but Amos had learned to recognize the signs of those merely pretending new faith in order to infiltrate his refuge house – long experience had taught him! A stocky man, Amos wore a large *baban riga* flowing gown and a colourful embroidered cap, a *fullah*, and sported a short, scruffy beard. He also bore bullet wounds, burns and lacerations that demonstrated the ongoing cost of conversion. He had moved his refuge house to the city after an attack, resulting in the death of one of those he was discipling.

Sometimes new arrivals would sleep in Amos's office for a week or two while he counselled and prayed with them. There was no room for uncertainty. But Amos knew the college staff and he knew about the college outreaches going on in new areas, and the large numbers of Muslims continually coming to Jesus in isolated provinces. He had already heard about the family John had helped to bring into the city for safety, and quickly agreed to take them straight to his home. John bought Amos extra beds for the family, and gave him some money to care for them. It would be subsistence living, but they would have food and shelter. They would be safe.

To be rejected from the network of family and community that underpins life in Africa and provides a safety net in times of crisis – but is unforgiving of dissension – and to be cut off from the *ummah*, the community of Islam, is almost unimaginable. It is terrifying, not just in the threat to life and the real possibility of economic destitution, but in the isolation from their family, friends, and all that they have known. The slow building into a new community of faith with love, with grace and, most of all, in truth, is step by step. Yet this new family was far more excited about this development of faith than they were mindful of the hardships. And they will be learning from those who understand where they have come from.

They will spend a year or more learning the word of God, learning to read and write – many come to the college illiterate – and acquiring life skills such as sewing, woodwork, or other trades that will help them to make a living. Classes are held in a corner of the small compound around Amos's house. A rough lean-to, with a rusty corrugated iron roof as its only shelter from the hot sun, it is surrounded on two sides by the compound wall, made of old cement blocks with a roll of barbed wire running along the top. Amos's wife teaches the refugees using a board made from a piece of plywood painted black. Those who live in the house, along with children secretly dropped off each morning by their Muslim mothers, sit at rough desks on cheap plastic chairs, or on a mat on the dirt floor. They have notebooks and biros and they learn in Hausa and in English. Everyone gets a Hausa Bible, which they find a real treasure.

The new family joined these classes. Their location will be kept secret. When they grow strong they will be witnesses to their own people of the astounding, transforming, liberating love of Jesus.

1.

A Firm Foundation

The Bible college in the north of Nigeria was founded in 2007 by a team that included John, myself, and my wife, Beth. However, when Beth and I first arrived in Africa in 1986, we would have been the first to admit that we were some of God's most unlikely tools. We could never have imagined that one day he would use us to build a college that would have so great an impact on so many lives.

We had felt called by God to come to Africa, where we joined Archbishop Benson Idahosa's Bible college. We quickly realized that we were out of our depth – we had no money, no church backing, and almost no experience. We had always imagined an Africa of quaint thatched huts. What we found was a slum. There were constant electricity and water shortages, institutionalized corruption was everywhere, and we struggled to adjust to a world full of noise, dirt and smells. Even the food – yam, the banana-like plantain, goat's meat – took some getting used to, and at the beginning there was not always enough to go round. We didn't speak any of the many languages we heard, only English, and our hosts, American missionaries, had enough challenges without a naïve young couple and their baby to look after.

All we had was God. But although it was tough, we were honoured to be a part of the work God was doing in the country. We worked, learned, and made ourselves useful in any way we could, by the side of a man whom the Lord used to change the faith landscape of the nation, which now has a population of more than 150 million. Benson Idahosa was a father in the faith, and kept us close to him as we grew. Literally millions of people were coming to the Lord as the Christian population of Nigeria grew from 30 to 60 per cent, in one of the fastest church growth periods in history. Our task, after some years, was to run the ministry's Bible college in Benin City, where the pastors were trained. It grew to accommodate 1,600 students annually from all over Africa, and thousands of them were sponsored by family and friends from our home country.

Through the Lord's power, the revival spread to many nations and transformed them. For example, in 1977 God had spoken to Benson Idahosa and told him to go to Ghana, which had been closed to the gospel during twenty-one years of communism. He arrived the next day and introduced himself to a Ghanaian pastor. As they drove through the capital city, they came upon a painter who had just fallen from a high building and was declared dead as he lay on the pavement. Many concerned people had gathered around. God spoke to Benson and he went to the man and told him to get up. He immediately stood up, perfectly well.

As a result of this miracle, Benson Idahosa was ushered into the president of Ghana's office that afternoon, and spoke with him and his cabinet. The president asked him to speak in the national stadium the next day, and promised to announce it on all Ghana's television stations. Hundreds of thousands of people came and saw God perform mighty miracles, and the gospel spread to the whole nation. In the succeeding years, we were among those who helped train over a thousand pastors for Ghana.

Revival and Islam

Understandably, the revival was not welcomed by Muslim leaders. Islam was originally brought to Nigeria across the Sahara in the eleventh century by the Fulani and Kanuri tribes, who converted under pressure from desert trading tribes such as the Tuareg further north. It spread by conquest – violent *jihad* – between the 1100s and 1400s, when the Fulani conquered and dominated the Hausa tribe. They then joined forces to subdue the tribes to the south, and formed an elite ruling class. In Nigeria today, the nomadic Fulani still raise cattle and sheep while the settled Fulani rule.

Islam has five pillars or acts of worship which all Muslims are obliged to perform: reciting the creed ('There is no God but Allah and Muhammad is his prophet'), the daily recitation of set prayers, fasting during daylight in the month of Ramadan, almsgiving, and pilgrimage to Mecca. Commitment to Islam as a way of life is required, following the law derived from the Qur'an: the *Sharia* law. Boys are taught to recite passages from the Qur'an in Arabic, from an early age. Understanding is not required – performing these rituals is enough. Morality, honesty, integrity, kindness and justice are not required for Islamic purity; ritual washing of hands and feet with water before prayer is said to cleanse them from sin. It is a righteousness of law, not of heart or of behaviour towards others. Lying or acts of violence are condoned if they further the cause of the *ummah*, the Islamic community. There is no personal relationship with God or assurance of salvation in Islam – it is fatalistic, 'as Allah decrees'. There is no concept of original sin or new birth. Allah is not approachable, and it is considered blasphemy to say he can be known. Because it is a lifestyle rather than a faith, it is almost always mixed with traditional beliefs and witchcraft, a 'folk-Islam'. There is no requirement to change one's beliefs or mindset; it demands only ritual performance and loyalty. In Nigerian Islam, as in traditional African religions, immorality of every description is rife.

The belief that the Islamic community cannot be ruled by a non-Muslim, or infidel, means Muslims must strive to dominate in a totalitarian form of government at all levels of society. Any family member who leaves Islam can be lawfully put to death by another family or community member. Islam expands into non-Islamic societies by *jihad* which is expressed at all levels, including blatant violence, academic persuasion and religious apologetics, working in all fields until Islam becomes dominant. Because it is perfectly acceptable to lie to a non-Muslim, the intention of domination is hidden until they feel strong enough.

Benson Idahosa played a large part in stemming the flow of Islam further south. Twice during our time with him, dictators declared by military decree that the nation was to become Islamic. Both times Idahosa boldly cancelled the decree on national television, instigating peaceful opposition and declaring, 'This nation will never be Islamic.'

With growing revival, the killing of Christians escalated in the 1990s, and Muslims believed they could take the nation while Christians 'turned the other cheek'. They assumed that Christians would just lie down and die, or that they would simply stop the revival. However, Benson Idahosa appeared on national television,

sharpening a large sword, and declared, 'I would like to
do a Bible study with Muslims. There is another verse
which states, "It is more blessed to give than to receive."'
They understood the meaning: Christians would not
give up the gospel, nor the nation, nor their children's
future.

A position of strength can save lives. But the real
strength of the people of this nation is their faith in God
and their determination to evangelize the lost. Christians
love Muslim people and reach out to them because of
this. When preaching the true gospel of Jesus Christ to
them, Christians come up against a system of false religion, lies and enforced submission. But if we do not
evangelize the people through the love and power of
God, the system and its adherents will tread us all under
their feet. As Jesus said, 'If the salt [loses its] savour'
(genuine Christian life and outreach) we are 'good for
nothing, but to be . . . trodden under foot of men' (Matt.
5:13, KJV). This is true on a global level. It is imperative to
take the gospel of Jesus Christ to the Muslim people.

Opportunities

During those years in the south, Beth and I developed a
heart for the north and travelled often to work with
graduates pastoring there. Before ghettoes developed,
Christians were not allowed to build church meeting
places, so had to meet under the shelter of bridges. In
one city, Muslims had often tried to kill or drive out
every Christian. One Saturday evening an announce-
ment to Muslims was made on television, that there
would be an anointing service the next day at 10, and
they must bring their anointing oil. This was code for an
attack on the churches at 10, and the 'oil' was their

weapons. Christian leaders answered with an advertisement the same night: 'We are expecting rain at our churches tomorrow: bring your umbrellas.' The Muslims cancelled their anointing services, not wanting to be dealt with by the 'umbrellas' (farming implements used as weapons). The majority of the population of this city is now Christian.

As the gospel has spread rapidly throughout the middle belt of Nigeria over the last thirty years, Islamic domination has gradually crumbled, as people come to faith in Christ and gain the courage to brave persecution from their families and communities. The middle belt, once dominated by Islamic elite resented by the community, is today largely Christian. Development, education and prosperity have slowly followed in the wake of Christianity, as churches are planted in villages and towns and community trust builds. However, the north is another matter: largely Muslim, with many places unreached by the gospel.

In Benson Idahosa's Bible college in the south, we opened a Hausa-speaking theology department to train northerners who travelled down for study. We attracted as many from the north as we could, to help open it up more to the gospel. The north was definitely where the need for future missions lay, and in 2006 we felt God calling us to leave where we were based in the south. We had worked with our pastor's ministry for twenty years, with 8,000 students passing through the college during our time. Those students now pastor thousands of churches in Africa and around the world. With God's help, we had come a long way, but he had more work for us to do. We left the Bible college in Benin City in February 2006, and began to pray about what we should do next.

Several opportunities arose. I was lecturing in the UK part-time on MA courses offered through a UK university.

Should we develop that ministry? A Nigerian leader with a prominent ministry in Eastern Europe offered me a position heading up a Bible college in a Western nation. Then friends from a large ministry in our home nation asked us to plant and oversee two or three Bible colleges in Africa for their denomination. They would fund it, which would solve any financial problems. But we had an interdenominational vision and believed it was a priority to maintain this. When we worked with Benson Idahosa in the south we shared a kingdom mentality, meaning we trained people from all churches. God is so much bigger than any one denomination.

I travelled to Cameroon and Ghana meeting graduates, and spoke in one church in Ghana which had 8,000 members. My friend, their pastor, oversees 300 churches and evangelizes internationally in Islamic nations; he asked me to lead his college and train pastors. I refused, telling him that I felt Ghana was blessed. It had good government, its infrastructure was good, and it was prospering. It had heard the gospel. It was not as unreached as other areas, not central in Africa, and not near great numbers of unreached Muslims, which was where I felt God wanted Beth and I to be. We knew we were being called to help those in greater need of support and encouragement, to train those who could reach others who have never heard the gospel. We knew it would be difficult; we would be starting something that was humanly impossible, but it was the right step to take.

Our family and friends had invested millions of dollars into the Bible college in the south of Nigeria and we left all of it there as an investment in the kingdom, to start again with nothing. We had moved our children to the UK for their high school education. Their school, where they received a full scholarship as a support to the work of God, had dedicated believers who taught there. (The eldest is now married and a qualified medical doctor. The next is recently qualified in medicine and about to get married. The third qualified in law, and is now studying theology, desiring to serve God in ministry. The next is studying law, and our fifth child is about to start vocational training.) We spent much valued time together as a family in the UK after their childhood in Africa, and we prayed over our next step.

The next step

In April 2006, Abubakar, a leader we had worked with in Africa for many years, came to the UK to do an MA in theology. At this time we had not yet seriously considered starting a new college in the north. Though this was our heart's desire, it seemed to us to be too large a step to take. However, before Abubakar came to the UK, others we had trained told him that God had called them to the north. They insisted that when we decided to go to the north, he must let them know. We had never mentioned this possibility to anyone, but by July 2006 we were convinced it was time to head north and start a new college. Abubakar then told us what the others had said, and asked permission to tell them of our plans.

We had worked with these people – Abubakar, Musa, Jacob, Phillip, John and Michael – for a long time, and so we knew each other well. They were all either ex-Muslims or had grown up in the north. God had formed an ideal team and brought them to us without us having to search. A friend called them 'the team you dream about having in the ministry'. Indeed, Deborah, the northern wife of one of our friends, had seen this new work in dreams, though we had never met her. After they married she told her husband, 'The Lord has shown me that a man is coming from another nation and is moving us up to the north where the Lord will do a work that will impact many lives.' We only heard about this after we had started the new college.

We needed an appropriate base for the new college, and the team agreed on a large city in the north, which turned out to be the same city we had prayed about. But how could we find a suitable campus there? Very few existing places, if any, would meet all the specific needs of a Bible college. Musa contacted the governor of that state, who surprisingly offered to give us land in the rural area he came from, just outside the city. However, we all prayed about it and together did not feel it was right, so we declined the offer. This turned out to be the right decision, as that particular governor was later indicted for corruption. (Musa is an invaluable team member. Growing up in the north, he was a committed unbeliever from a nominal Christian home near an Islamic-controlled city. His sister, a Christian, began preaching to him, annoying him. He decided to read the New Testament to learn enough to defeat her arguments, but by the time he reached the book of Acts, he found that he believed. He immediately started preaching to his family and went on to work with an evangelical church, preaching the gospel from village to village, and establishing churches. He was used by God in leadership roles in the church's operations in his region before we met up with him in the early 1990s, when he came to the Bible college in the south of the country.)

The team kept searching for the right place. Phillip travelled to the city to look for buildings to rent. He visited his sister who lived on a medium-sized estate, and she told him about the main building on the estate, an abandoned conference centre. This building was ideal: it had room for classes, student boarding facilities, a library and offices. It needed a lot of work to make it ready for occupation, but it was otherwise perfect. This was the only complex in the city that suited our needs, and we were led straight to it.

The owner was a Muslim leader in the city, an *alhaji*, which meant he had been on pilgrimage to Mecca. He had been involved in a planned attack against Christians which broke out two days before 9/11 in New York in 2001. Many Christians and pastors died in a two-week killing spree. However, he claimed to have changed, and offered us the building for three years, but we would need to have the money to cover the rent.

Just before Christmas 2006, our team and their families loaded their belongings onto a large truck and headed north. Night driving in Africa is dangerous – visibility is poor and serious accidents are common. Heavily armed bandits, sometimes from other nations, lie in wait to rob and kill travellers. It isn't uncommon to have to wait in villages as Special Forces travel ahead to 'clear the road'.

We drove through the day and night, arriving early in the morning. By then, and just in time, we had the money for the first rent payment. Rent is required a year, sometimes two years, in advance, making this a significant amount of money. We parked outside the building and called for the landlord, hoping the building was still available. He came with the contract; we signed it, and moved our belongings inside. There was a lot of work to be done. We painted the inside of the building, made tables and chairs for students, bought beds and mattresses, repaired drains, installed toilets and bathroom doors, and bought a big tank to collect water, as the flow from the town water supply was intermittent. Two days later, someone moved out of a nearby flat on the estate and we took possession of it for a staff family. Within a week, enough houses on the compound had become available for the staff and their families to be settled. We bought chickens and rice, and celebrated Christmas together while continuing preparations to open the college by the end of January. God had met every need.

In January 2007, the college opened with thirty-three full-time students. A few months later, we asked the landlord to give us the dilapidated unused mosque in the corner of the compound, which had been partially demolished by angry locals in retaliation for the 2001 riots, to convert into a rudimentary kitchen where staff would be able to cook the students' meals each day. Another building on the estate had previously been occupied by Mormons, who had paid the rent for two years in advance but abandoned the building soon after we started church meetings in the Bible college hall. We moved in and divided it into more classrooms and hostel space.

We were off to a miraculous start, the Lord leading every step.

2.

Growing in Faith

The college is a place of worship and study, of fellowship, nurturing and work, where people are prepared by the Lord to fulfil their calling to know him and to be a blessing to others. The staff and students care for each other, whilst focusing on reaching out to those who have not yet heard the gospel.

The overriding culture in the Bible college is that of Jesus and his kingdom. Visitors who enter a room where staff and students are talking often cannot tell which is which. They get along as equals, yet with mutual respect. Staff play table tennis with students, or volleyball and football on the weekends. At other times they go out together to evangelize in people's homes, or to preach in open-air meetings in market-places.

In a society that is less private than in the West, there is a much greater ease in sharing faith in public places, including on public transport and in workplaces. The gospel spreads much faster in this type of culture. Personal space is not an issue. Neighbourliness is a common attribute of African society. No one says, 'This is mine alone' – it is a sacred duty to share all you have with others when needs arise. People are responsible for each other.

Home visits are part of daily life, whether to pray together, to share the gospel, to inform people about an upcoming meeting, or just to hang out; no one waits for an invitation. There are no expectations except of a welcome. There is an understanding that you share what you have, and do not worry about what you do not have. We are all family in Christ: this is not an academic statement, but real in practice. To say 'sorry, no room, too busy' is just not something that happens in Nigeria.

The college is a family. Both single people and married couples with children enrol as students, and live on the campus in boarding facilities, or in flats nearby. The children of students and staff are passed from person to person, juggled and cosseted, or toddle up and down the aisles between desks in the lecture rooms, or church pews, kept safe in the midst of all the activity going on around them. Children are loved and treasured as gifts: 'Children are for all of us', as the African proverb goes. Married couples use family planning to control the size of their family, but to wish for a family without a child is incomprehensible. The antics of children are a joy that all share. The young men handle small babies just as competently as the women, and little children exude confidence and security (and often mischief) as they are assured of boundless love. The family structure of African society is real in the church, and very evident in the college.

In the college there is a real sense of freedom; students discuss the Scriptures and theology among themselves. They readily ask questions in class. They have a great hunger to learn and to grow. They come from different ethnic groups, different religious backgrounds, different denominations, and different nations. They are different ages and they speak different languages. They encounter new customs for the first time, and eat food they are not used to. Patience with others is developed in this way.

The teachers sit among the students. A staff member or a student will share the word of God, often a student translating from English to Hausa, or the other way round, with others chiming in to correct any mistranslation, and there is always a readiness to receive it all without offence. In this we grow together.

Chapel services and special meetings begin with exuberant praise. Simple songs mixed with classic hymns which expound the gospel, and songs in Hausa and other African languages, with Fulani or Hausa-style dancing, reveal a faith that is personal and relevant. The worship and singing in the services is naturally expressive and free. It does not have to be whipped up. In Christ we know freedom; in contrast, Islam means 'submission'. But we love because he first loved us. We follow Christ's example, who laid down his life for us. This is what others should see in us.

Vibrant preaching in chapel services and inspirational messages about faith and missions build strength into those who are taking the gospel to others. Prayer meetings can be short, or go on for hours, and even overnight. Prayer is real. There is nothing like persecution to make your prayer life serious! At other times, professionals visit to speak on their area of work, or heads of denominations teach systematically through the Scriptures. Students speak in chapel, and share testimonies of God's grace day by day.

Students work as well as study in the college. They clean, help prepare food, maintain the equipment, film the services, edit the film, work on the radio talk-back programmes (where people phone up and ask questions on live radio, every Sunday afternoon for an hour), repair electrical appliances, run power generators, serve as librarians, and do the groundwork for pastors' conferences or outdoor evangelistic programmes. None of these things could be achieved without everyone working so hard; it prepares them for ministry.

Each weekend they collect water from a nearby well – a simple hole in the rock with a metal cover – and wash their clothes. There is no dress code, no conformity to peer group. Students wearing African dress, T-shirts or suits and ties sit side by side and no one thinks this odd. There is no need to dress like others to be accepted, and we encourage people to do what is right, from the heart. The focus is on Christ renewing the heart, with discipline and leadership where needed. Students are quick enough to correct immodesty or excess in their own ranks. Respect for others permeates the culture of the Bible college.

Students prepare for Sunday services by practising with the choir, often a new song one of the students or staff has written, or by visiting nearby homes to invite people. Each of the leaders of the college pastors a church in or near the city. Students help out in these churches, visiting homes and taking on administrative tasks. It is good training for their future. By the time that they graduate, each student has been involved in starting a new church.

The faith of the people is simple in that there is such gratitude expressed to God and to human beings for every blessing received. But when it comes to teaching, they (including the uneducated) can grasp new concepts far quicker than classes in other nations. The uneducated are generally very clever! This is just their first opportunity for formal learning, and they blossom.

The college runs a two-year diploma programme, teaching in the Hausa, English and French languages. Students take parallel classes in different rooms according to the language they speak, with lecturers and staff for each language. Hausa is spoken by many millions of people in the nations around us, and French is spoken in some of the nations from which the students come. Some students are illiterate and are taught first to read and write Hausa, then English. There are not enough books in Hausa, so English helps the students to develop in time. Each student is an individual with their own needs and issues, and each requires a lot of time, effort and patience from the staff to help them grow. They have as long as it takes.

The college also runs a two-year degree course, following on from the diploma, with qualified lecturers from several other universities and denominations working with the staff. Qualified and born-again staff, truly inter-denominational, is a great blessing. God has used many denominations, and each one has something unique to offer. If we cut one denomination off, we lose what they have to offer and become a little more isolated. We need balance as we seek to maintain a biblical approach rather than a denominational approach in teaching.

Each day the students have classes and library study periods. The library is large and students sit in personal cubicles to read a wide range of quality books, which includes works from different periods of church history as well as study guides, or watch teaching seminars in one of the personal television booths. They research online and write their assignments on computers. The generators run up to fifteen hours a day at the college in order to provide enough electricity to power the equipment. For most students, college is a steep learning curve: not only the content of the courses, but the technology that they are using. It is new to many, but they are sharp, and with the right direction and guidance from the staff they pick it up quickly.

Michael, the librarian, was born to a Muslim mother and Christian father, and worked as a pastor for a number of years after his graduation from the college in the south. He spent his early years with his maternal grandmother in a village, so his education automatically consisted of reciting the Qur'an. He eventually entered formal education, in an Islamic primary school, when sent to stay with his father. Later he was withdrawn and sent to a Christian missionary school in the north of the nation. 'I cannot say whether I was a Christian or Muslim then,' Michael says, 'but the truth was I did not know Jesus and I was not born again. A pastor visited my secondary school and spoke about the sacrifice of Christ. I felt the touch of God. I lack the right words to describe the sudden change that occurred within me, but whatever it was, I loved it.'

Students need the best education for ministry, just as a doctor or lawyer would. They also need Spirit-filled lecturers. The college must be accountable to the wider community in its standard of service and hold government accreditation, but first of all it must be biblical. Being biblical doesn't just mean getting it right in our study, but that we actually follow Jesus and do his will. It means that Christ bears fruit in our lives and relationships with one another. This must take first place.

Matthew's story

In the first year of the college, I was working at my desk when a graduate from our days in the south walked in with a tall friend. My office desk was in the library, which was good for interaction with the students, and allowed easy access to the books for study.

The graduate introduced his friend, Matthew, who wanted to enrol in the college. After a short conversation with Matthew, I knew that he would face some challenges in the college, but just referred him to the registrar's office. He was from a part of the country where doctrines of demons are prevalent. When a church member buys land, a pastor says it must be anointed with oil or holy water to deliver it from demons, or a curse would follow. The pastor demands money to do this. Large sums of money are raised this way, and many pastors live in luxury in contrast to the poverty of their surroundings. They protect these teachings jealously, preying on the ignorance of great numbers of people. Coming from this background, I could see that Matthew would struggle. I was leaving the country that day for a time, so left the matter in the leaders' hands and said nothing about it to them, but expected they would have trouble teaching him.

When I returned, I heard from some lecturers that Matthew would often stand in class and ask questions. At times it would seem aggressive, but he had a genuine desire to learn. Our lecturers were patient with him and answered from Scripture each time. Slowly Matthew was learning. Our lecturers work hard to bear with and nurture each student in this way, no matter what it takes. Each one has to be treated as an individual.

Later, we had a visit from a graduate I had seen two years earlier on my last trip to Cameroon. After opening six successful churches, this graduate had fallen into sin and was forsaken by the Christians. He had to return to his Muslim people for food and shelter. He went back to the mosque, while in his heart praying to Jesus. The Muslims said, 'He is a pastor and will not be with us long' while the Christians said, 'He is a sinner and God has forsaken him.' We had spoken together about this in

Cameroon for about three hours, but I was surprised to see this brother in my office. He told me that two weeks after we had prayed together in Cameroon, God had spoken to him and restored his faith. He was sent to work in Nigeria, and now oversees a different group of churches. I was delighted. He told me that this time it would be different: he had made a more serious covenant with God than before, and he would not fall again.

He was shocked when I said, 'That will not help you.'

'What do you mean?' he asked.

I told him about Peter's experience when he fell and Jesus said to him, 'Peter, I have prayed for you that your faith will not fail. When you are restored, feed my sheep' (Luke 22:32, our paraphrase).

My friend from Cameroon began to cry, tears flowing down his cheeks as he heard Jesus' words. He recognized the unconditional love of God for him, and that it was God alone who held him, nothing to do with the intensity of his feelings, and that it was totally beyond his ability to keep his side of the bargain. Jesus would keep up both sides: then it would work.

When I shared this in the class, I noticed Matthew. A breakthrough in his understanding was happening – for as I spoke, he saw that *God* has the power to transform us, to make us new; that it is not our seriousness but *God's grace* that keeps us walking his way.

About three months later, he stood in chapel and said, 'I would like to give a testimony.' He walked to the front: 'When I came to the college, I knew everything. I had started churches, done many outdoor preaching crusades. I had worked with this and that ministry. But when people ask me when I was born again, I tell them that it was here last year.' His whole personality had changed. He was now gracious and a lot of fun to be with. He also works day and night serving the college and is currently an assistant lecturer.

It is not common for a student to say they were born again in the college, but it is common for the realization and revelation of Christ to grow and replace a foundation of self. This is the most important work of God in preparing us to fulfil the Lord's purpose. He gives us stability in faith.

The staff

All the staff continue to grow in their education, and are enrolled in accredited programmes of study in different nations. To be viable in the long-term, the college must have the best accreditation so that we can charge higher fees when the students are able to pay. This provides funds to sponsor students from the grass roots level, who cannot otherwise afford it, and keeps us on track as a missionary institute. For the long-term sustainability of the work, this balance between quality of education and missionary focus is essential.

Visitors from other nations enjoy meeting the students as they work alongside them. Our daughter served in a local hospital, and our sons made tables for the office and bookshelves for the library. Other visitors helped set up the primary school and assisted in the library; others worked with the computers. Some of our visitors have been to the state deputy governor's house for dinner and prayer. They stay in our guesthouse and go on tours of the local zoo and wildlife park, and admire the state's scenery, from beautiful mountains and waterfalls to picturesque villages and farming districts. They buy local batik cloth, leather goods or woodcarvings, while making friends with the Christian and Muslim craftspeople.

As a staff team, we enjoy a level of peace and fellowship that is precious. Visiting heads of institutions say the love between students and staff and the lack of politics are unique and must be maintained. The staff never say, 'That is not my job', but pull together for the goal of glorifying the Lord. They work with students, washing clothes and dishes, cooking and farming. They share the load at home, changing nappies and bathing children. Husbands and wives encourage each other, each developing their own areas of ministry.

The team display different gifts. Abubakar is a gifted team leader. His example creates a culture of kindness, faith and diligence within the whole ministry. Musa, the registrar, is a gifted Bible teacher, bringing out gospel truth in the local context. Jacob, the dean, has a dedication, work ethic and care for the students that brings a solid foundation to the college. Phillip, the academic dean, is a backbone in the college, both academically and as college builder. John is the evangelist, who hates sitting at an office desk! Michael is a leading degree lecturer, librarian and a 'Barnabas encourager' to all. They all bring different characters to the group.

The staff has grown to include many other teachers, administrators and pastors. The additional members have taken on the knowledge of the word of God that the founding team have taught them. The college itself is a team. Whether students, staff or international friends and partners working together, the love of God shines in our hearts through Jesus Christ, and we want this love to reach many, many others.

3

Open Arms

The city where the college is located is well known for its hospitality, and there was no exception made to this rule in our case. The people and churches received us openly and warmly when the college started. In the first year, we put on a small pastors' conference, and despite spending very little on advertising, we were surprised that pastors came from twenty different denominations. We began to hold these pastors' conferences at regular intervals in different northern cities, and in Chad. In all of these places, our college graduates lead churches. A graduate in Chad, for example, oversees 150 churches in the nation.

One city had just experienced a major attack against Christians and, as a result, pastors cautiously gathered there for a three-day conference – it was a good time to encourage the churches. Between meetings we went to visit the leader, or king, of that state. He received us in a very grand room, whose walls and ceiling were panelled with polished carved woodwork. The room contained a lot of fine local art, as well as expensive carpets and elaborate furniture carved from the best local timber. He motioned to us to take our seats, while his subjects sat on the floor around him.

Seated on his throne, the king asked when I was born. He was obviously older than me, but when I told him my age, he said that he was born in 1976. Everyone looked perplexed, but I knew what he meant and explained: 'He is speaking of the year he became king.' The king was surprised, and asked how I understood this. There are a lot of similarities between African cultures and the Hebrew culture, and I told him that the second psalm (the coronation psalm) speaks of Jesus when he was begotten (crowned) King of kings. From this point, the king was open to us and we were able to share the gospel and pray with him.

Following this, we were led by the Lord to begin plans for a larger pastors' conference, to be held in our city in 2009. I had been praying about this when a graduate, Dominic, visited us. Dominic grew up in the semi-tropical region, between the north and south of the country. He came to meet us to share his concern about the church's deviation from the gospel when dealing with traditional religions. Ancestral worship and spiritism were enshrined in traditional African religion before the gospel came. Spiritism refers to the belief that the physical world can be controlled by manipulation of spiritual power, and the ancestors are entreated for assistance in controlling spirits. 'Do not eat this or the spirits will afflict you' -such knowledge is gathered through life's experience. It can be based upon truth, referring to an animal found dead, which could pass on disease, or it may simply be based on superstition. The same superstitions from the past exist in Western cultures. Some of the traditions are similar to Old Testament restrictions, and were handed down by caring parents to protect children from harm.

Many of these cultural practices reflect genuine care for people and substantial knowledge of the environment –

such as which plants treat various illnesses – so it would be foolish for outsiders to discount all of this cultural wisdom.

However, it is the mixing of spiritism with the gospel that causes problems. In Christ, we live by faith, while superstitions bring bondage and corruption. In the past, some African independent churches have been known for this mixing, but in recent times Pentecostalism has also strayed in this way. Some teachings on spiritual warfare are based on spiritism; this has become a concern, as this cultural perspective has been used to attract members into churches or to make money. This 'defining the gospel by cultural values' is common around the world. For example, 'pastors' claim they have special powers to bless you if you give them money or buy an anointed stick, garment, water or oil. They warn of curses, sickness and death for people who do not give. They claim that by fasting and giving money, people can break demonic powers, gain wealth, or have their enemies die. A whole system of works-based religion is built that supplants the gospel message: this is a demonic attack against the church.

Knowing the temptations that the graduates face in their cities and villages, I was praying about this when Dominic arrived in my office. Dominic pastors a church in a city a full day's drive away, and caught a taxi especially to meet us to deliver the following message: 'In our city and in many other places, pastors are going astray. Many people in their churches are being led away from the gospel. You have trained pastors who are working in cities and villages all over the continent. The Lord wants you to gather them together and encourage them. They need follow-up and help.'

Acting on this message as guidance from the Lord, we announced a pastors' conference for June 2009.

Abubakar, the college leader, invited guest speakers – local leaders of evangelical mainline and Pentecostal denominations. We met with local pastors, and made plans to contact those outside the city. Without the funds for large-scale radio, television, or printed advertising, we were assisted by people who volunteered to travel to a few cities outside our state to inform others of the proposed conference.

We had no idea whether people would attend. But at the close of a meeting where the new governor of our state was present, he walked over to me: 'I hear you are putting on a conference. Thank you for what you are doing for our people. Would you like me to attend?'

'Certainly we would!' I said. Surprised and gratified, I added, 'We look forward to seeing you there, sir.'

A month before the conference, pastors began to send in their registration forms, and by the time the conference started, 2,000 registrations had been received. Many of these pastors worked in villages with little or no cash economy, often farming to feed their families. They wanted the same thing as every other family: a good education and a future for their children, security for their old age. But for these things they had to trust God. Obtaining the transport fare to the city for the conference, and credit for their second-hand pay-as-you-go mobile phone was as much as many of them could manage. Some of them were educated, but forgoing comfort to stay in villages and help their people. They could not afford a steep registration fee. Most could not afford a hotel and some, not even food. They ministered to people whose offerings came in kind, and they did not have much to spare; there was certainly no budget for conferences. It is an honour to help these people, as the body of Christ is worth it. If the body of Christ is worth dying for, it is worth living for.

The conference delegates started arriving in our city. Some moved in with our friends and staff for the week. We filled the college dormitories and laid extra mattresses on the floors of the classrooms to accommodate village pastors, and as these filled we hired cheap hostel accommodation in the city for those who came from all over the north and nearby nations. Buses were hired to transport delegates to and from the rented meeting hall.

The students were part of the workforce. Each day, two simple meals were prepared by a small army of cheerful helpers. Students put out 2,000 chairs and erected canopies, printed 2,000 spiral-bound copies of teaching notes to give out to delegates, ushered and sang in the choir at the meetings, and stayed up at night serving food and cleaning up. They worked around the clock the whole seven days of the conference.

Staff member Phillip was constantly on the move, directing students in their tasks, collecting urgently needed supplies, and working closely with team leader Abubakar to ensure the smooth running of the conference. Phillip grew up in military establishments in different cities across the north; his father was a ranking officer, a Fulani whose own father was among early converts from that ethnic group. His father's position allowed Phillip access to good schools. Although dragged along to church and associated activities all his life, Phillip gravitated to bad company and was not impacted by the gospel until he experienced a radical change of heart at a campus Christian outreach at the polytechnic where he was studying. (His background means he can join in with appropriate banter and successfully bargain with the Muslim traders, and he is an asset to the college.)

Somehow, all the arrangements for the conference came together. From unexpected sources all the funds necessary came in to look after over two thousand people for a week, and to manage all of the logistics.

The state governor came as promised, a dignified elderly gentleman, an evangelical brother in the Lord, humbly paying his registration fee and wearing his delegate badge, sitting on a cheap plastic chair like everyone else. When his turn came, he spoke for two hours, from Paul's letters to Timothy, holding the rapt attention of the whole group. The deputy governor, a devout Christian Catholic lady, spoke on loving our enemies, which seemed to be received with caution by the delegates. (It takes on a whole new meaning after so many attacks for so many years, but remains an imperative command, which God gives us the grace to obey.)

One of the other speakers was an Anglican bishop, who so appreciated the meetings that he later asked the college to lead an Anglican clergy retreat. The Anglican archbishop was invited to lead the delegates in communion but was unable to attend, being outside the city at the time. Highly regarded, he has stood steadfast in the gospel, while he and his family have come through unspeakable sufferings at the hands of Muslim terrorists.

We prayed for a lady senator who came to the conference from another state. Joyful, gifted and strong, she was the first Christian senator and the first woman senator from an intensely Islamic area, her life at risk every day.

The state governor gave every delegate transport money to get back to their village, which the college staff distributed to each delegate in need. Reporters from television stations and the federal national radio carried news of the conference nationwide, for free.

This was a first for the region: all denominations gathered in one place in fellowship; so many coming together; so many pastors and missionaries working in remote, Islamic areas encouraged and helped in their work; a state governor preaching such a biblical and challenging message to pastors. We joined together to pray for gospel outreach in the Sahel and for the state governor, knowing the challenges that lay ahead.

The mission of the college is to encourage people to boldly push northward with the message of eternal life. The miraculous intervention of God in this conference emboldened us to go on.

4.

Reaching the Unreached

Mission stations are a crucial way of getting the gospel into unreached areas. A simple worship centre and accommodation for pastors (usually college graduates) are either rented or built. This becomes the hub fellowship. Using bicycles or small 100cc motorcycles to go where there are no access roads, just rough tracks, the pastors evangelize interior villages, starting home meetings in satellite towns.

Evenings are spent sitting under the stars by cooking fires, talking to the elder and his brothers, or to the wives and children. During the day, pastors work beside the people, farming with hoe and cutlass, forming mud bricks, or making grass thatch to repair houses and grain stores during the dry season. Sitting under a thatch lean-to, or maybe under a mango tree, by a compound fence of woven grass matting strung up to keep the goats out and toddlers in, the pastors share a simple but powerful gospel message. Inside the fence is a cleared open area surrounded by huts: possibly four for the wives and their children, one for the man and a couple of others for stores. (Traditional villages, those which are not near a road for passing trade but reached by a simple footpath, are generally composed of a number of such compounds

positioned fairly close together for safety.) The pastors
are invited to share a drink with the villagers, or a meal
from a central bowl, everyone seated on mats and eating
with their fingers. The cooking is good in areas where
supplies are at hand, and eating in this way is relaxing
and enjoyable. The Bible is then taught and literacy classes might be held. The local culture is often very pleasant
and hospitable, but extreme poverty, pagan depravity
and Islamic control bring destruction to individuals and
to families.

Islam was not strong in this part of Africa until the second millennium AD. The Hausa people began to convert
to Islam, but were forced fully into Islam through the
jihad (holy wars) of the Fulani people. The Hausa/Fulani
then formed a pact that has dominated much of the
region ever since. Their influence extends across the
Greater Sudan, the Sahel and the sub-Saharan belt. There
is an Arabic/Berber mix in these people groups, similar
to the Tuareg people from whom the church father
Augustine came. These people groups have important
links to the ancient church. Before Islam, the gospel was
widespread and reached West African regions along the
trade routes across the Sahara from the north.

Today, things are changing again in this part of the
world. In the nineteenth and twentieth centuries, missionary movements set up thriving churches among the
indigenous people groups, but the main Islamic peoples
– the Kanuri, Shua Arabs, Hausa and Fulani – were
largely untouched by this Christian influence. In the
1960s, a huge gospel movement gained momentum in
the south of Nigeria, and after many years the inevitable
impact of this is being felt further north in this sub-
Saharan region. Today this is a significant area for the
church and for Muslims. The college team is determined
that the region will become an exporter of the gospel of

Jesus Christ, rather than an exporter of Islam. God has a gracious plan to exalt his name and greatly expand his church in this area, which is already seeing large numbers of people coming to Jesus.

Yusuf's story

One such person is Yusuf. He grew up in a remote region, where nothing much had changed for centuries. Recently foreign Islamic nations have increasingly promoted the building of mosques in isolated places, like Yusuf's town, as part of the global expansion of Islam, assisted by the abundance of petro-dollars. With the growth of the gospel, Muslims have realized the importance of areas they had previously ignored. In the past, they were happy to leave people in these places to paganism and concentrate their energies on the cities, but as the pagans began to turn to Jesus they became educated, integrated and active members of the nation, slowly bringing development and prosperity.

Yusuf is the son of the local emir, or king, and his family had converted from paganism to Islam. This Islam, as in most places, was a folk-Islam, retaining the local flavour and spirit manipulation (magic) as part of its belief system. One commentator has said of Islam that it 'flows like water', meaning it fits in with the local culture and little, if anything, is changed. While morals are espoused in propaganda, in reality multiple wives, instant divorce for the male, honour killings and abuse of little girls are common, and in private homosexuality, rape, HIV and drunkenness are rampant. All that is required is that adherents follow the confessions and rituals of Islam.

But the ritual requirements are absolute and merciless. Yusuf's family demanded that he follow their conversion.

Yusuf was disturbed. Something was stirring in his heart that would bring a sword to his family, as Jesus said in Matthew 10:35,36, where one would be divided against another – but eventually and irresistibly it would bring true salvation to many of his relatives. Looking up at the sky and contemplating God's creation, Yusuf prayed to the creator: 'I want to know you. If Islam is the right way, put a love for it in my heart. If Jesus is the right way, put a love for him in my heart. Do this within three days, so I will know it is from you.'

The third day after his prayer, Yusuf experienced the love of Christ for the first time. He knew an overwhelming love for Jesus deep inside. He experienced true fellowship of the Spirit that was not manipulative or controlling for selfish interests, but which lifted him from the heart to act with truth, integrity and energy in service. He could not deny this complete change: he knew it was in answer to his prayer.

This sealed his direction. After seeing the light so powerfully, he could not turn away from it. No matter what the offer or the threat by his family, Yusuf would follow Jesus Christ. His parents were outraged. They locked him up, held him in chains, refused him food and threatened to kill him. His mother attempted to poison him. His father disowned him. All his property was confiscated. He was beaten with heavy sticks, but refused to renounce Jesus.

When too weak to be held in confinement any longer, he was freed, but kept in the house. When partly recovered he managed to escape, making his way to the state capital. He looked for a church, finding a small Christian meeting place hidden behind houses on the outskirts of the city. From there he was put in touch with a pastor who took him on a two-day drive to the south. He stayed with a church, lost in the large urban sprawl, and remained hidden for eight years.

Yusuf served the church and worked in the city while he grew in the Lord. The Christians there cared for him until the call of God led him back to the north. His pastor said he must go to a Bible college and led him to our college. Yusuf enrolled in the diploma course and he is now in his third year, studying for a degree. Since being with us, he has visited home a few times. He is careful, but has not been arrested, mainly because his mother and one of his brothers have now also come to know the Lord. They have been instrumental in reversing the dominance of *Sharia* law in their town.

Yusuf's heart is now very much to see his family and community come to know Jesus Christ as saviour, and the college staff saw this as a God-given opportunity for bringing the gospel to these people. By December 2009, we had already started a mission station in Yusuf's town. A handful of people had come to know Jesus, pastors were working hard in the region, and the church was ready for growth. I went to visit Yusuf's family, as a courtesy call to establish a relationship. Yusuf took us to the home of his elder brother, now the emir since his father had recently died. We arrived just at the time of evening prayer, so sat down to wait under the shelter of a canopy against the wall of the emir's house, opposite his mosque.

A mud building rendered with cement and unpainted, with a tin roof and a small porch, and plastic water pots by the entrance for ritual washing, the mosque was easily identifiable by the horn speaker nailed to the outside wall. There was a much more elaborate mosque in the centre of the town with a minaret and speakers broadcasting in Arabic five times every day, financed by foreign Islamic nations.

We watched as the emir and his elders removed their shoes, washed their hands and feet, entered the mosque and stood in front of their prayer mats. They recited in Arabic and then knelt down as a sign of submission, their heads touching the mat.

When finished, they came out and sat down with us, the emir on his throne, while I was seated next to him as a guest of honour. The town elders and the college team sat on chairs or on the carpet and the mats. After a long and gracious ritual greeting, we offered a sack of rice as the traditional gift. We thanked them for their cooperation in setting up a church and an adult literacy class. They hadn't actually helped, of course, but at least they had not opposed us. They expressed their pride in Yusuf's progress and their gratitude that this honour was coming to their town, hoping a school and clinic may one day follow. We prayed with them, in English, Yusuf translating into Hausa, and then we were invited to visit Yusuf's mother.

In a windowless mud-brick room, with a compacted earth floor and an old piece of cloth nailed up over the entrance, we met Yusuf's mother and the other women, seven or eight of them, ranging from teenagers to very elderly, all wives of Yusuf's father, the previous emir. The new emir was now responsible for their care. Some carried babies on their backs, tied on with faded African cloth. Others had small children on their laps. The younger wives were nervous, while the older wives looked more relaxed as we greeted them. They responded shyly, some smiling cautiously under their *hijab* headscarves, replying in subdued voices, and motioning with their calloused hands to their chests as a sign of greeting and welcome. Poverty was evident everywhere, even here in the emir's compound. We talked a little while through an interpreter, and then prayed with the women and children. Not many visitors to the emir would have bothered to meet with them.

It was already dark, and time to leave for the planned evangelistic event arranged for the town centre. We joined the rest of the team, where the outdoor meeting in the main street was under way. Bible college students had put up advertising posters around the town earlier in the week, but angry Muslims had followed behind the team, pulling the posters down and stamping them under their feet. That night we preached the gospel to over four hundred people with loudspeakers, and prayed for the sick. Perhaps another 1,000 people unavoidably overheard that gospel message. There was no opposition. The local people were amazed, and they asked, 'How is it that you are so bold?'

Fruitful

The emir's brother (another of Yusuf's brothers who is now a believer) gave us a plot of land and buildings to use for a mission centre. Regular church fellowship meetings are now held there. The morning after the town event, people came to the mission centre secretly, like Nicodemus when he came to see Jesus by night (see John 3:1–21). One Muslim man came in through the back entrance of the compound. After looking to see if anyone had followed him, he said quietly, 'I want to know Jesus.' The pastor spoke with him and they prayed together. As he left through the front entrance, one of his wives crept in through the back. When she left, her son followed behind. None of them knew the others had come. The next day the pastor went to their home and started a house fellowship there. The head shaman or witchdoctor of the town also asked for a house fellowship to be held in his home, for he and his whole household had come to know the Lord. This is how the gospel is spreading through the town and neighbouring villages.

There are places in this part of the continent where people still live most of their lives naked and without the trappings of 'civilization'. They have not yet been reached by Islam or Christianity, and there is no education or infrastructure. They are just known as 'uncivilized' pagans. Visitors to villages like this are confronted with extreme poverty and depravity. In Yusuf's town, thousands of people gather from neighbouring villages once a year for a pagan festival. Frenzied celebrations are held, and young girls, not yet even 10 years old, are forced into marriage with older men. Our pastors were able to preach at the last festival, and those who came to faith returned to their communities to spread the gospel through more house fellowships, regularly visited by the pastors.

Three of our pastors work in this mission centre, reaching out to these neighbouring villages. One of them is married and houses his family in a nearby city where they can educate their children, as there are no 'book schools' in this town, or in any of the villages. Over the years, we have helped to train more than 8,000 pastors who are now working all over the continent. Encouraged to greater boldness, some of these have come north to join in this groundbreaking work. They are zealous and hardworking, skilled and Spirit-filled. They are bold, they know the Scriptures, and they are fruitful in the gospel. They do not mind the harsh conditions and it is an honour to be working with them.

'He spends all his time with the enemy'

After preaching in Yusuf's town, we left for the state's capital city, reaching it at about 11 p.m. – there was no curfew in that state. Along the way we drove through multiple military checkpoints. Some of the soldiers were drunk, and all were heavily armed, but they were all pleasant. We slept the night in a guesthouse run by a Muslim. The other guests were mainly Muslim politicians and businessmen. There are around twenty pastors we have helped train working in this city, and a couple of them visited us that night at the guesthouse. They pastor different churches, and one of them runs a school for 450 students. He declared it a Christian school, but Muslims are welcome if they read the Bible and pray Christian prayers during assembly. They come to the school to be educated, but are then being saved.

The next morning we left early to visit another mission station. This town, an important market centre situated on a significant river, has previously experienced many deadly attacks against its Christian inhabitants. The state capital dominates the region's indigenous population, and in recent years hundreds of Christians in this town have lost their lives. Kazeem, the pastor who started this mission station, is one of our college graduates and a Fulani convert with a strong desire to reach his Fulani people with the gospel, many of whom also live in this area.

Many Fulani walk their zebu cattle north in the wet season to escape the tsetse fly, and then south in the dry season to locate water supplies. Fulani are present in large numbers across nineteen different African nations. By the 1800s they shared control of various states in West Africa. Predominantly and proudly Islamic, they seek to maintain their ethnic and religious purity, along with political control, wherever possible.

Working from this mission station, Kazeem spent many hours sitting with Fulani leaders, discussing the gospel. We bought him a small motorcycle and he often travelled far from the town, locating large Fulani settlements in the bush. Kazeem joined the people in caring for the cattle, ate at their campfires and slept in their shelters of sticks and dried mud. Fulani often regard their cattle more highly than their wives. According to *pulaaku*, the Fulani strict system of ethics, cattle are considered to be more valuable than non-Fulani people. All this changes when the Fulani are saved for Jesus Christ.

Fulani are handsome, tall, and often distinctively dressed. The women use henna to blacken their lips and wear beads in elaborately braided hair, with necklaces, earrings, nose rings and anklets. Kazeem looks and dresses like the Fulani men, in a long colourful gown. Eventually the Christians in the town became suspicious of him. They complained to us, 'He spends all his time with the enemy, the ones who have attacked and killed so many of us in the past. We do not trust him. He is one of them.'

It is unfortunate that the Christians in the area do not reach out to this 'enemy', the people who do not know Jesus. They consider them unworthy of the gospel because of what they have done to the Christians. This view is understandable because of all that they have suffered: it is like the early Christians not trusting Saul after Jesus called him on the Damascus road (see Acts 9). But it is a great joy knowing Fulani cattle herdsmen are hearing the gospel message in their own language.

Churches in this region have kept their faith over the years, and so to keep the peace we moved Kazeem out of this town and another pastor moved in to take over the station. Kazeem has now gone to open another mission station in a different state. Last year, he went to Libya to preach. His heart is to reach Muslims anywhere he can and God is using him. He is intelligent, with a university degree in chemistry, but he wants to go where the gospel has not yet been. This is the greatest desire of us all. How can Christians sit down and do nothing when, despite the darkness, the love of Jesus is so easily transferable to others? We can only achieve this with God's help, but salvation is a miracle and there is nothing easier than a miracle. 'With man this is impossible, but with God all things are possible' (Matt. 19:26, NIV).

5.

Sovereign Intervention

No one comes to know Jesus except by God's own hand. This is nowhere more evident than where believers are persecuted for their faith. When he calls people, he gives them the faith to stand their ground, and fulfils his purpose in them.

Fatima grew up in a rural region dominated by savannah and a hot semi-arid climate, close to one of Africa's strongest Islamic cities with a population of about 10 million. In recent years other Islamic nations have financed this city to make it a stronghold of an expanding Islamic influence on the continent.

Fatima helped her family by farming groundnuts and fetching water from the wells, and joined in annual Ramadan festivals, celebrating the original revelation of the Qur'an, and the *Qurbani Eid* (or *Eid Al-Adha*), commemorating 'Abraham's offering of Ishmael on the mount'. She watched as several village leaders were sponsored in different years and flown to Mecca for the annual *hajj*. Her region considered itself the strongest and purest Islamic region south of the Sahara, and deviations from the faith brought swift punishment.

Twenty-five years ago, when Fatima was married, she was asleep in her home when a man dressed in white appeared to her. He said, 'I am Isa (Jesus). I bring you truth.' She woke up the next day, a new person. Her husband recognized it immediately, and threw her out of the house. Her instantaneous rejection was a great shock, but she could not go back and deny the truth. The villagers also said she must leave. She walked alone down the long hot dirt track to reach the main road to the city. The Lord comforted her and said he was sending a woman to look after her.

When she reached the tarmac road, she spotted a car pulled up by the roadside. The driver, a Christian woman, was having engine trouble. Fatima stopped to help and together they got the car started. Before this driver had set out that day the Lord had spoken to her, telling her he was sending a lady she would look after. She knew Fatima was that person and asked her if she needed a lift – quite a risk for a Christian to take unless they know it is from the Lord! So on the first day of her new faith, Fatima was on her way to a nearby Islamic city to live with her new friend. The lady discipled her and Fatima spent a year in her home, learning the Scriptures.

This wonderful mentoring period was not to last. At the end of that year, an attack against Christians broke out and Fatima's friend was among over two thousand people murdered. However, she had sown seed into Fatima's life that would bear much fruit. Her faith strong, Fatima returned home to her village, hoping she could spread the gospel.

Although the village community allowed her to stay, she was not reunited with her husband. For ten months she was persecuted for her faith, from beatings to being denied basics rights, such as permission to buy or rent land for farming, access to the village wells, or food beyond that which sustained her life. She grew weak under the persecution and considered renouncing Jesus.

She prayed, 'Lord, this is not helping anyone. No one is being saved. It would spare me a lot of trouble to say I do not believe in you any more.' But the Lord answered, telling her that he had a purpose, and that she should be patient a little longer.

Two months later, something happened that turned things around. One of the young women in the village had been chronically ill for a long time with an unknown disease; there was no doctor to diagnose the illness and no cure for her ailment. No treatment available helped her. The villagers called in the traditional healers, the old women with knowledge of herbs, and the witchdoctors, but they could do nothing. The Islamic clerics came to pray, but this did no good.

Fatima heard the people of the village talking: 'We will ask Fatima to pray and see if that helps.' She did not want anything to do with this – she was in enough trouble already, and if the lady was not healed when she prayed, things would get even worse for her. But the elders insisted. So Fatima went to the young woman and prayed that the Lord would heal her, in Jesus' name. Ten minutes later, the woman, who had been bedridden for months, was up and cooking food for the people of her house. That day sixty-four people in the village became Christians. Fatima's former husband was not among them. She has remained unmarried since she met Jesus.

People were being saved in nearby villages. Not all of Fatima's disciples are open worshippers; some come at night and meet outside the villages for Bible studies. Thirty churches have now been started in this Islamic district, all overseen by this strong woman. (We know several women whom God has saved and is using to boldly spread the gospel where angels and men would fear to tread! They have kind hearts, but they are also resolute for the truth and immoveable.)

A visit to Fatima

We paid Fatima a visit. En route to the village, we passed through towns where the atmosphere of aggression sent shivers up our spines as Muslims glared in our direction. A simple roadblock on our way out would easily allow them to seize our small party. But we put that out of our minds as we continued on the road which haphazardly meandered through village after village.

The anger displayed towards us seemed at harsh variance with the neat, beautiful environment. The contrast of colours made a striking setting: the tawny mud-brick huts with their thatched roofs, the lush green of the maize crops by the dusty road . . . Many of the villagers carried farming tools, or balanced firewood or bundles of yams on their heads, all modestly dressed in brightly coloured flowing African clothing, the women with headscarves, and the men with soft fez caps. But joy was absent from their faces, and the reality of their harsh lives was never far from our minds.

In each village we saw a mud-brick complex with a corrugated iron roof and a large cross of unfinished wood on the side of the building. These were the church meeting places that Fatima was overseeing. Her boldness and courage was (and is) highly admirable. At any time there could be an attack against this growing Christian community.

As foreign visitors, we were not in as much danger as the people there. If there was to be a negative reaction against our brief stay, it would most likely be directed at Fatima's church after we had left, yet they were eagerly awaiting our arrival. (Indeed, the Bible college's partnership with Fatima may help the gospel spread even more. People are impressed that international visitors come to see the Christians in their villages.)

The gathered congregation were singing when we arrived in Fatima's home village, where an interpreter, an architect who supports her ministry, had driven for three hours to be there to help with the meeting. Some churches in the nation that are keen on missions support village pastors with motorcycles, or pay them a small wage to enable them to establish and maintain churches in outlying places. Fatima is known and respected by a few churches far off that help her in this way, assisting pastors serving in the churches she has established. During our visit we spoke to the congregation, and before leaving promised to do what we could to support the work.

Sharia

Over the years, Fatima has been imprisoned on different occasions and tried in *Sharia* law courts on the charge of converting Muslims. Every time she replies, 'I haven't converted anyone. Jesus has done this, and he brings them to me and I look after them.' She has been flogged on several occasions, but each time she has finally been released.

Sharia law stems from the belief that Islam should control every area of life. It is the application of Islam to human relationships, business and daily life, a little like the Old Testament Judaism from which it is derived. A lot of the tenets come from the Hadith, Islam's second most holy book, which interprets the Qur'an for daily living and activities. *Sharia* is therefore very ancient in its code. Subjects such as the treatment of women – who have few rights and are regarded as property – and the punishments, such as amputation, castration and stoning, seem to come from a tribal society where the concepts of justice and equality do not seem to exist. For example, a man may have four wives at once, and he alone can apply for divorce. Non-Muslim communities within Islamic jurisdiction must pay a ransom or price per head, a tax to avoid the forfeit of their lives and property. To shame your family is a capital offence, as is leaving Islam. Under *Sharia* law, Fatima is guilty of both.

The federal secular constitution trumps local *Sharia* law, often giving Christians respite from the strictures of Islamic law. For example, in the college there are a number of students who have been sentenced to death by the *Sharia* law courts of the Islamic religious police in their local government areas, for the crime of leaving Islam. Having sought refuge in our city, they will not be prosecuted as we do not have *Sharia* law in our state. In their home states the judgement has been passed, there is no appeal, and they could be executed by any member of their family or community with complete impunity. However, if they could find a police station with non-Muslim police brave enough to resist the resulting riot, even in their home state, they could appeal to Nigerian National Law, where freedom of religion is a right under the Nigerian constitution. Sadly, the local police are not usually able to resist the pressure of the violent Islamic community (see Author Note at the start of the book).

Like Paul

When I first met Fatima, we communicated through a Hausa interpreter. Although we could not speak directly and had grown up under the most different conditions and influences imaginable, in opposite parts of the globe, our fellowship in the Lord was instant. She struck me as being a bit like the apostle Paul – one who would stand up for her right to spread the gospel. Seeing her strength, I felt sorry for any who would dare to stand in her way!

Many of the pastors who now work with Fatima and help oversee the churches trained at the college. The Christian children in her community were being persecuted in their local school, so we bought her some land and built them a Christian school. Fatima is just one leader in this part of the nation whom the Lord is using like this, all seeing similar breakthroughs. In every case, the Lord is working sovereignly and miraculously in revealing himself to many Muslims.

6.

Fearless Love

Pastors we have helped to train work in and around the main city centre of Fatima's region. Each one has a story to tell, and many of them are as remarkable as hers. For example, Yohanna, a converted Muslim, has lived through several attacks in that city. Hundreds and, at times, even thousands of Christians died helplessly in each attack. The Christians and southerners in this northern city are forced to live in a ghetto; cut off from the facilities everyone else takes for granted, they are deprived of fresh water and electricity, and rubbish piles up in the streets. Grouped together as they are, they also present an easy target during the frequent attacks. They decided they would defend themselves, so they prepared home-made firearms and waited. The next time they were hit, they stood their ground against surprised attackers.

The last time we visited that city, we held a pastors' conference with the college team and an international guest. We often hold these conferences in northern cities to encourage pastors from all denominations. Between the meetings we spoke with a Pentecostal bishop who is a friend and a father-figure to younger pastors. He described the atrocities committed against Christians, and his near-escapes while protecting church members. The brutality is unimaginable. The bishop now sits on a government-appointed committee, along with other ministers and concerned Muslims, trying to bring peace to the region. He could live in luxury in the USA, but he is called to stay and help.

During one attack, Yohanna received a call on his mobile phone from a pastor who was trapped inside his house with his wife and children. Muslim mobs were rampaging from house to house, boarding up the windows and doors and setting the buildings alight with petrol bombs, burning everyone inside. If anyone tried to escape, they were cut down. Yohanna put on old army fatigues from the days when he was a soldier, and drove into the battle zone. Pretending to be a Muslim army officer, he got the family into his car and took them out of the city. One error and they would have all been killed. When safely out, Yohanna received a second call, so went back to rescue another Christian family.

His denomination later transferred him to our city, where he pastored a church. Attacks hit his district once again. I visited him there and walked around the streets looking at all the burnt-out houses and hearing all the stories about his church members, yet there was not one complaint from Yohanna. So many we know have risked their lives for Jesus and his people. Others have been killed.

One of our graduates now pastors with the Anglican Church. His house near the college was set on fire, with him and his family inside. They hid in an underground room; although they lost all their possessions, they were safe. They still live in the city and are still reaching out to others with the gospel. What is so incredible is the emotional health of the Christians; they are happy, faith-filled and bear no animosity. Their desire to reach the enemy with the love of Jesus is unabated.

Our city is a hub where students come to train. Situated centrally, it is easily accessible to significant northern cities as well as the populated rural areas of subsistent agriculture between them. One of these cities has around 1.5 million people, with large populations of Kanuri and Shua Arab. Recent statistics have stated that there are just a few Shua Arab converts to Christianity, and that from some millions, only twenty Kanuri have come to know Christ.

The Kanuri have been Muslim for 1,000 years, and although they led a powerful empire that reached its height in the sixteenth and seventeenth centuries, they are not the original inhabitants. The original inhabitants of the region resisted the Kanuri and other Islamic groups in their attempts to convert them. The first settlers were long ago influenced by Christian Nubian kingdoms, in upper Sudan, before the process of Arab domination and enforcement of Islam resulted in the eventual overthrow of the Christian Nubian rulers in 1504. More recently, a freed Kanuri slave who had become a Methodist minister was the first recorded modern missionary to the region in 1884.

Jacob's story

Jacob, a member of the college team, is a native of this area, from one of the non-Islamic groups. In 1923 a Brethren mission was set up, slowly expanding among Jacob's people, who were initially resistant to the gospel because of resentment that the colonial authorities had placed them under the rule of Islamic Kanuri. Sudan Interior Mission and Sudan United Mission also set to work in the area, reaching other indigenous groups who had resisted Islam.

With repeated attacks from Muslims and little protection, centuries of domination by Kanuri and Shua Arab have made the Christians tough. When attack threatens today, Jacob is ready to defend his family, home and friends. He grew up in a nominal Christian family. His local area is full of beautiful countryside, rich in agriculture, and the people are hard workers who make the most of their farmland. Jacob was saved at a youth meeting after the pastor pointed to a cross, saying, 'The Jesus you see suffering there, did this so that you could be saved.' This caused Jacob to spend a sleepless night. He prayed that Jesus would save him from the sinful life he had led, and from that time he began to experience peace and a freshness which has grown over the years as the word of God has transformed his life.

Sarah's story

As part of their study, students of the college undertake periods of practical ministry. Sarah, a degree student at the college, is married to a pastor in a predominately Muslim city in Jacob's region, and returned there for her practical ministry period. Sarah was determined to share truth with the Muslim people there who need the love of God. Each day she tied her lively 2-year-old son, Seth, on her back and went from house to house, preaching to Islamic women and their families. This was at a time when Christians in the city were under heavy threat.

A group called Boko Haram was killing both Christians and police. Translated, this name means 'Western education is a sin'. Boko Haram was led by an extremist whose aim was to stamp out non-Islamic schools and universities and the police force which he felt was anti-Muslim. His group went around attacking churches and killing

Christians, but then they attacked a police station and killed several officers. The police finally acted against the group and announced they had wiped out the problem. They surrounded the compound where Boko Haram were holed up, allowing only the women and children to leave before launching an attack. It was during this time that Sarah was visiting Muslim homes in the area, sharing the Scriptures and praying with the women and children. The women responded, 'We believe what you are saying. We know Jesus is the truth. We want to follow you, but if we do, our husbands will kill us.'

On their return journey to the college, Sarah and her son were travelling in a ten-seater taxi van (a '*tooki tooki*'), crammed in with about twenty other passengers. The Holy Spirit gave her a strong urge to preach and she began speaking out loud in English. Some in the van were afraid of the boldness of her Christian message, thinking it would stir up trouble with the Muslims, but when the journey was finished a passenger approached her and asked her to repeat what she had said in a language he understood, Hausa. He was an Islamic scholar and wanted to accept the gospel.

Sarah returned to the college and began work on her written project – about the need for churches to support members who are widows. In the local and Islamic cultures in that area, when a man dies, his property goes to his brothers and the wife becomes destitute unless she marries her husband's brother. In her project, which will be taken to churches in her city, Sarah encourages Christians to stand up and ensure they do not adopt this part of the local culture.

We thank God we have had a part in training about forty pastors now ministering the gospel in Sarah's city. They have lived through much persecution. They pastor churches which between them have thousands of members, and serve as chaplains in one of the best hospitals in the nation, as well as in the army. They operate schools, conduct missions into villages to reach Hausa and Kanuri, lobby politicians, and publish books to raise awareness of their plight: their church members are discriminated against in employment and are denied city amenities, from water supply to electricity and education, and are forced to pay higher prices for many goods at the market.

Other Islamic nations have financially encouraged local authorities to ensure that Islamic domination continues in the region. This is done by implementing *Sharia* law, preventing villages that are not strongly Islamic from developing economically (denying access to schools, clinics, water, electricity and other services), and ensuring that non-Muslims do not gain representation in state politics. These sanctions are not based on ethnic affiliation, but only upon adherence to Islam.

Deborah, one of the college staff, was living in Sarah's city during an earlier attack. Many churches were burnt and pastors murdered. She was teaching in a school with around a hundred small children in her care. They heard the sound of riots and saw smoke in the sky. The other teachers fled, but she could not leave the children. Deborah started calling parents on her mobile phone, and within an hour she was able to clear the building and flee to safety. All of the staff – college administrative and auxiliary staff, and teaching staff – have gone through this several times, but they are the most hospitable and kind people, even with the harsh conditions in which they live.

Ibrahim's story

God is reaching the extremists, too. Some have become students in the college. Ibrahim lived in a different city in

the north-east of the country. He joined one extreme fun-
damentalist Islamic group after another, seeking the way
of truth – he thought that if he became totally committed
to Islam in this way, he would find it. He started and
operated four Islamic schools; one was attached to his
house, and he spent most of his time searching the
Qur'an.

Ibrahim had no Christian witness in his city, where
there were seventy mosques but not one church.
Nevertheless, the Holy Spirit began drawing his attention to references to Jesus in the Qur'an. The Qur'an says
that Jesus (Isa) is the highest in heaven, above all the
prophets. It says that Jesus never sinned, but all the
prophets had sinned. The Qur'an is not inspired by God,
but God has ensured that it does contain some true state-
ments about Jesus (as well as some false ones), as
Muhammad was influenced by the Christians and Jews
of his time.

Ibrahim was determined to find out more about Jesus.
He saw that the gospels of the New Testament were also
mentioned in the Qur'an. Ibrahim wanted to get these
gospels and find out what they said about Jesus; this was
how the Holy Spirit eventually revealed Jesus to him.
Today he is serving the Lord, discipling other Muslim
converts in refuge houses. He wants to go back to his city
and open the first church in that place.

While he was studying at the college, Ibrahim
received a phone call saying if he wanted to see his
father alive he must come to the hospital that day or it
would be too late. This is sometimes a trick to lure converts back home to be captured, but this time it was true.
Ibrahim did not have the money to go and so he said, 'I
can pray here as well as I can there.' The next day I was
in the library when I heard Hausa students rejoicing.
When they get excited they leap up and down like

antelopes, whooping loudly, laughing and singing. Ibrahim had received a call saying his father was healed, had seen Jesus and was now a believer. He was an imam (an Islamic leader) and influential in politics in his area. The governor of his state had been working on plans for him to build an Islamic education centre. His salvation would make waves!

In every place the faithfulness of God, the growth of the gospel and the miracles of salvation in both ordinary and influential people are apparent. This rapid spread of the gospel is a major reason for the Islamic persecution that this area is experiencing. But believers are greatly encouraged to see God so powerfully and graciously revealing himself to people and totally changing their hearts.

7

Practical Ministry

During their training, practical ministry periods test the students' mettle. They learn Arabic while in the college, and some graduates from previous years minister across the Sahara in northern Africa and the Middle East. Their training prepares them to preach in difficult places. Students go out from the college preaching the gospel and helping in churches, where they are a blessing as they grow in understanding and in confidence. They are mentored by pastors who help prepare them for their future. Their stories give a glimpse of life in this part of Africa.

Ahmed's story

Ahmed is a Fulani student. His family are cattle herders with a strong and proud Islamic tradition. African missionaries went into Ahmed's region to preach a few years ago, and met strong resistance to the gospel. Other missionaries in the region asked them to tone down their message for fear of trouble, but they insisted on preaching the gospel plainly. So the local king, the traditional ruler who still commands significant local authority, called a council to expel all missionaries from his realm.

During the proceedings, the king's son was born again and the next day addressed the council: 'We have heard about Muhammad, and now we need to hear about Jesus.' The king changed his mind and decreed that the missionaries be allowed full access throughout all the villages.

Ahmed was one of those who heard the word of God and was saved. Immediately his family rejected him. He was stripped of his inheritance, and his wife was taken from him; all his property was confiscated, and he was forced to flee to find help from other believers. A few years later, he came to the college to study. After a year he wanted to go back to his town and witness to his faith, so during the practical ministry period Ahmed set off for home in a taxi van.

News is sometimes slow to travel, so Ahmed did not know a riot against Christians had started in his home town. Angry Muslims kicked up dust and fired bullets in the market-place, and their frenzied shouting terrified the stallholders and townspeople. Ahmed had hitched a ride on the back of a goods truck for the second part of his journey and arrived in an alley close to the market. Climbing down from the sacks of vegetables and stacks of yam, as the truck's diesel engine cut out, he heard a roar. The angry mob, recognizing him and knowing he was a Christian, cried out, 'He is one of them!' Before he could escape they had grabbed him, forced an old car tyre over his head to pin his arms to his body, and poured petrol over him while screaming, '*Allahu akbar!* Burn him, burn him!' It seemed his short life was over.

However, while they were trying to light the petrol, a stranger escaping from the chaos in the town centre on a motorbike saw what was going on. He forced his way through the furious mob, aggressively thrust Ahmed's captors aside, grabbed him, and dragged him onto the back of the motorbike. Before the mob realized he was not one of them, the stranger had escaped and was skilfully negotiating the narrow alleyways of the crowded township, through to the roads beyond and out of reach of the rioters.

Ahmed spent the next three weeks preaching the gospel in the same town, staying in a pastor's house on the outskirts. The rioting and killing stopped after a few days. Those who had been part of the angry mob went quietly about their daily business, but unprovoked animosity seethed under the surface. Ahmed helped out in the local church, preaching alongside the pastor, visiting house to house and sharing the gospel in the Fulani cattle-camps just outside the town.

Ahmed's family knew he was in the town, as he had contacted them earlier. He had heard that his father was very sick, having been confined to his bed for some time. He wanted to visit, but was forbidden by his family (supported by the Islamic community) to go to his father's home, so he prayed with his pastor, left the matter with the Lord, and went on ministering to others. Just as his ministry period ended, Ahmed received a message. A delegation of extended family members had discovered where he was staying and were asking to see him. They told him that his father was calling for him to come to his home. When he entered the bedroom, his father greeted him in a friendly manner, asked how he was doing at college, and then asked Ahmed to pray for him. Ahmed prayed, talked for a while, and then left to return to the college.

Students return from their practical ministry period on the weekend, ready to start classes on the Monday. This time all returned safely and began the week with an exam, before settling into their usual routine. The following week, Ahmed stood in class and asked if he could give a testimony. Despite having nearly being killed, he was obviously very happy. He explained that two days after arriving back at the college, he had heard that his father was healed. He then received calls from his three brothers, each saying they now wanted to hear the gospel. Ahmed was exuberant, as were all of the students. Dancing broke out in the class, and students carried Ahmed on their shoulders in a procession of joy, holding Bibles aloft, singing.

Risikat's story

Risikat went to a different region for her practical ministry period, but also met opposition to her message, from Muslims and also from some of the Christians. (Sometimes, where a necessary breakthrough cannot be achieved by religious 'works', but by Christ alone, the message is resented.)

Serving as an assistant pastor in a local church, Risikat did housework, helped on the pastor's small farm, counselled and prayed with believers in the community, evangelized in homes, and led prayer meetings with the church. One Sunday the pastor also asked her to preach.

As she preached to a small congregation of twenty people that morning, a man suddenly stood up, brandishing a large knife, and came towards her. Without time to think, Risikat commanded the man to stand still. He froze where he stood, so Risikat continued her message. The man did not move for the next twenty minutes. When she finished speaking, Risikat walked over and prayed for the man, as tears rolled down his cheeks.

While this was happening, four people came in, carrying a young woman on a stretcher. They told the congregation she was dead and there was nothing they could do to help her. The pastor did not know how to respond, so made an excuse and left the church with his two elders. This left Risikat there with the pastor's wife and the small congregation. She went over to the girl on the stretcher, and told her to get up. She stood up, healed! This caused such a stir in the town that the church doubled in size in one week.

The next day a family brought a young girl to Risikat, saying the child was possessed by a demon. They had made the girl fast for weeks and then tried to beat the demon out with sticks. Risikat spoke with the girl for a while and then told her parents, 'Your daughter does not have a demon. She was just disobedient and has promised to change.' From then on there was a change in the girl.

The following year, the pastor of that church came to enrol in the Bible college.

Through Christ alone

The students are just as surprised as anyone else at what the Lord does. They return from their practical ministry sharing their experiences with each other and with the staff, happy to see what the Lord has put in them through his word during their classes.

The first few months in the college are a trying time for some new students. If they believe they can help themselves, this is challenged by the gospel. One student cried out, 'But you are making me redundant!' The lecturer answered, 'Yes, you've finally got it!' We cannot achieve anything through our own works, but through Christ alone. When they see the power of God in their practical service, they know it truly is the Lord's work.

8.

Courage

Stories of conversions in this part of Africa demonstrate the nature of the gospel. The altar call approach is not usually the way people come to Jesus. It is difficult to say to a Muslim, 'All I am asking is that you accept Jesus' when in fact we would be asking much more than that. We would be asking them to forsake all they have: wife or husband, children, family and property, and to risk losing their life.

There is no difference, really, between true discipleship in Africa and anywhere else in the world, but here it is easier to see. 'Easy faith' is a false gospel. But when God changes the heart, we are ready to count the cost, because of the reality of Jesus within.

The college must maintain gospel outreach to marginalized people that are not being reached. It is the gospel that changes the heart, and when worldly values cause many to be ashamed of the gospel, we must keep our focus. The gospel is the only hope of the individual and of any nation. The New Testament emphasizes the need to preach the gospel where Christ is not known, remember the poor, plant churches, train leaders, and occupy all realms by praying for the government and by involvement through effective apologetics.

Benson Idahosa, the pastor we worked with in the south of Nigeria, built hospitals and academic institutions, which was the right thing to do. However, these had a relatively small impact on the nation; it was the gospel proclamation in his calling that fundamentally transformed it. When people abandon the gospel for public credibility or tax deductible benefits, we must not follow. One foreign government said they would support the development of vocational education in another nation, but not religious education. They did not understand that it is education in godliness that builds a nation.

A region must change from the inside; it cannot come from foreigners on the outside. This is why the power of the gospel is the essential factor in personal and regional transformation. The task of the college team as helpers is to equip locals at the grass roots level. When God reveals himself to others, it is our duty in love, and our joy, to work alongside them. This means equipping them to fulfil God's purpose for their life, and to reach their area with the gospel.

The stories from our students that follow reflect what the Lord is doing in the villages where the majority of Africans live.

Yakubu Bukar

I was born in a Muslim family, and grew up with an uncle who was a fisherman on Lake Chad. I was a fanatic and spent much time reading the Qur'an. I preferred speaking Arabic as 'God's given language'. A friend was trying to read the Bible to me, and although I refused to listen, I had peace about what he was saying. He said I could have his Bible to read after my normal Muslim prayer, and that I should ask God to show me the way to salvation.

One day I read it and prayed and experienced a change. Soon after I had a dream in which I was in the sea, helpless, but somehow my feet found the ground. Then I was hungry and a tree grew and started producing fruit of two different types. Then I saw three stars, which called my name and said, 'You are the man God appoints. He will use you to deliver your people who do not know me.'

I got up and prayed the Muslim prayer. At 4 p.m. the same day I had a vision: 'Do not forget the covenant you have with God.' I decided to travel to my family's home in a different nation, seeing that God wanted to use me. Reaching the area, I first stayed with a minister of Christ for nine months, and then I travelled to my family home.

When I arrived, my younger brother opened my bag and saw the Bible and some Christian books. He took them to my father, who said I should leave his house since I was no longer a Muslim. I did so, staying with friends, but after some days he pleaded with me to return. I did not know he planned to set my hut on fire with me inside, but through God's mercy a friend warned me. They burnt my hut that night, thinking I was asleep inside. Friends helped me to get transport money. I left, and received help to stay in a refuge house. Eventually I came to the college.

Samaila Bala

I once heard the gospel, but I considered it to be false and a fairy tale. A year later, I had a week of sleepless nights. On one of the nights I saw a vision. I was told that I should not joke with the message of Jesus, and that it is the message that will bring me to life. The next morning, I went to my mother to seek advice. I told her that I wanted to be a Christian and that I wanted this matter to be between the two of us, so that my brother should not hear about it.

She began to recite Islamic religious incantations, and accused me of wanting to spoil the family name: in that region we were a notable family in the Islamic religion – a family without Christian testimony. I begged her not to tell people, but after I insisted on following Jesus, she raised her voice, calling on people to come.

My brothers and neighbours came and the place became chaotic. Some were suggesting that I should be killed, while others were saying that I should be taken to the emir's palace. The local emir is my brother. On reaching the palace, they advised me to recant my intention of becoming an infidel. They released me and I went to the *madaki* (the emir's assistant, an inherited position), who was a Christian. He was afraid and asked if I was serious, because being a Christian in this area is difficult. When he realized I was serious, he phoned a pastor, who said they should move me away to avoid a problem with the Muslims, insisting that it be done at night. The *madaki* therefore hid me in his house till nightfall.

Without notice, there was a summons from the palace to the *madaki*. The emir told him to bring me to the palace, accusing the *madaki* of setting out to convert me, to spoil his family name. The *madaki* said he had never spoken to me about becoming a Christian. The emir told the *madaki* to produce me, or be removed from the *madaki*ship.

The *madaki* said, 'If it is the issue of the *madaki*ship I can step down, but honestly, I have never spoken to your brother about becoming a Christian.' The *madaki* was hoping that because I and the emir were relatives, I would be safe. But the emir said he should set aside the issue of us being relatives.

The *madaki* came home and told me I must be brought
to the palace. Otherwise his house would be searched
and if they found me, it would be torched. He said if I
truly wanted to be a Christian, whatever people wanted
to do to me, Jesus could avert it. I told him that if I went
to the palace I would have to recant and become a
Muslim or they would kill me, but through his persist-
ence I eventually followed him. On reaching the gate I
saw a crowd. When they saw me, they started saying
they would kill me. Some did not even want me to be
questioned, in case I recanted and was allowed to live.
When my other brother heard, he came with a cutlass
saying, 'Allow me to kill this infidel before he destroys
our family name.'

The emir asked me why I had betrayed their trust. I
said, 'I stand by what my mother told you.' An Islamic
cleric slapped me. The emir said they should be careful,
as there were youths outside with weapons and if they
came in, they would have a murder case on their hands.
Someone else took a cane and began to beat me with it.

I considered my uncle, who normally lived in another
town, to be a wicked person, but my escape came
through him. He arrived in the evening and entered the
palace asking, 'Where is the infidel?' The emir asked
again if I would recant my earlier intention to be a
Christian, but I said no. He then took the horsewhip
from the palace attendant and started whipping me. But
my uncle said, 'In today's world we cannot easily kill
him, as there will be trouble.' He advised that everybody
should leave the palace, while they determined what to
do.

My uncle took me to his home in another city. On our
way, some youths threw stones at the vehicle and broke
the back window. My uncle asked what had made me
want to become a Christian: 'Is it a lack of money? Did

the Christians give you money?' He said my family would take me to traditional or psychiatric doctors, because it was a demonic attack. He told me that if I insisted on becoming a Christian, the holy book said I should be killed. He gave me an opportunity to think about it till the morning, but God worked his miracle for my escape. When I think about what Jesus did for me at that time, I am always encouraged.

Early in the morning I heard the garage door open and my uncle drove in. He asked if I had said my prayers this morning. I said yes. He said that was good, as it meant I had come back to my senses. He thought I meant the Muslim prayer. He then said that I should take my bath and prepare to return to the village. Later he called me to tell me the governor of that state was sending him to attend a meeting, so he could not take me back to the village that day. That is how God performed his miracle. My uncle said he would ask his driver to take me to the village, and advised me to tell them that I had said my Muslim prayers in his house. He added that if I insisted on becoming a Christian again, they would kill me. As he left, he gave me some money.

After eating, I went to the gatekeeper and said I wanted to go out for a stroll. He said he had been told not to open the gate for me until the driver came. I persisted until he finally opened the gate. When I knew I was out of sight, I ran to the main road and flagged down a commercial motorcycle, which took me to the Federal Polytechnic so I could see my sister.

She did not know what had happened to me. She had become a Christian seven years before. When I told her my story, she raised her hands and began thanking God, and later began to cry, saying that God had started to do his work. She said I'd called her an infidel when she became Christian, and that there would be trouble if I remained there, because they would look for me in her house. She took me to a pastor's house where I confessed and received Christ as my Lord and Saviour. I was then taken to another city, and then to another mission station in a different state and, after some time, was eventually brought to the college.

Since coming to the college, I heard that my sister was taken to a main centre for further questioning concerning my whereabouts. They threatened her, to find out if she had seen me. They took her to a mosque and told her to place her hands on a Qur'an and swear that she did not know where I was. She said to herself, 'In the name of Jesus' and laid her hands on the Qur'an and said she did not know where I was. She told me she was pricked in her conscience for lying, but she said it to save me. A pastor had to secretly come to her rescue.

After almost two years, I still cannot return to my town. Whenever I am discouraged in my Christian life, I find strength in what my older sister has done for me, to continue in the faith. This I know: it was not my wisdom or knowledge that has done all this and kept me thus far.

Yusuf Itiya

I was converted in a Muslim college, a Qur'anic school, but my teacher did not know. I went into a trance and I saw flames, and Jesus appeared and told me the fire was for my family and me. As I was crying, I came to understand that it was only a vision. I went to the Muslim teacher and told him what had happened. He said I had sinned, and that was why I had had this kind of vision.

Another day, Jesus appeared again and asked me to believe. I said I was afraid because if I became a Christian I would be killed. I told him that my uncle was killed as a result of being a Christian. Jesus said he would take me to a place where no one could touch me. So I went to the teacher the second time, and told him everything that happened. He told me that it was all a lie and that I was still living in sin.

The third time Jesus appeared he said from henceforth I should not tell anyone of my encounters with him, unless I met a pastor or a Christian who was ready to pray with me. So I became restless and I did not tell anybody about it. From time to time I kept hearing his voice and all the things he said to me, but was not able to tell anyone.

One Friday after the Muslim prayer, I decided that I must believe, even if they killed me. I went to visit a pastor and we prayed together. My friends found out and went about telling people of my conversion. From that day, my parents began to search for me in order to take my life. They sent a message that they were going to capture me and lock me up in a cell. I had to leave the town.

I have been kept safe by pastors who have looked after me, although my father is still searching for me. I believe that God will not leave me until he has fulfilled his purpose in my life. Even if they arrest me today and kill me, I know that I am saved.

Aminu Dauda

When my father was younger, he was sent to some missionaries to be taught to read. It was expected that he would eventually preach the gospel. But the gospel never took root in his heart. In 1999, when he was older, he asked some Christians if their church would come to his home town and establish a school to teach his children. There was no school, no electricity, and no development in the town.

They came and started classes to teach literacy. All of my father's children were taught to read and write in the Hausa language, but I was separated to be nomadic, to take care of my father's cattle, as we are Fulani. I would spend days away with the cattle before visiting home for food supplies.

I went home one day and saw the visitors teaching my brothers and sisters. I sat far off, but was listening. One of the teachers asked who I was, and whether I was a member of the family. My family said my father had instructed that I should not be taught. My father was afraid that I would become a Christian, because of dreams that I had told him about, where in a vision I was telling my family to accept Christ. (I had these dreams as a child, when I did not know Christ.)

I was fascinated by what the visitors were teaching, and often crept there so that I could learn something. I stored it all in my memory, and when I returned to the field I practised writing on the ground. That is how I learned to write.

One of my older brothers was given a book containing the gospel of John. I entered his house and stole the book so that I could read in the field. I read the whole of the book, which changed my life. I could not perform the Islamic rites as I used to do any more. Whenever I visited home, my father noticed that I did not say my Muslim prayers. I told him I always said my own in the field.

The time came for me to let it be known that I had received Jesus Christ, to no longer try to hide my faith from my father and my family. It was 2002 when my father decided that my younger sister (a Christian) should marry a Muslim whom she did not like. My father beat her because she would not marry. She then ran away and has not returned since. This made my father angry. He reported the matter to the *yan da'awah* (religious police). They supported him in telling the visiting teachers to leave.

Then my father came to the field and told me that if I renounced Jesus he would give me a car and the whole herd of cattle. But I said I only wanted Jesus Christ. He devised various ways to discourage me from following Christ, but to no avail. He was afraid to kill me because when I was a boy he gave me charms, and he thought I would use these against him.

He called people and told them to cast a spell on me and make incantations to kill me. He contacted a witch-doctor to execute me. My father saw that he could not succeed, but still threatened to kill me if I did not renounce Jesus Christ. My brothers also rejected me. I continued to live for almost one year without a place to stay.

Some years have passed since then and I am now training in the college. So far, six of my family have become Christians, and a church in my area now has forty-five members. I am hoping to go back to the church and be their pastor. Meanwhile, my father does not know the whereabouts of my sister. I am intending to bring her to the college to be trained.

Samaila Adamu

I started *makaranta* (Western education) in a primary school. One day while throwing stones, I accidentally hit my friend in the eye, so I had to run into a tall field of guinea corn to escape retribution from his family. I decided to end schooling from that day, and asked my parents to send me to *makaranta allo* (Islamic school). I was there for almost four years until a famine in 2003 sent me home.

One day as my uncle, a Christian and a prosperous irrigation farmer, went out to work, I decided to follow him. I used to observe his behaviour, but he never spoke to me about Christianity. As we walked to his farm, he began to speak to me about how the Islamic religion started in our town.

I went back to the Islamic school, but within a few days I felt I could not continue there any longer. I called a bicycle rider to take me home on the back of his bike, but before we started our journey I saw my uncle's son and we talked for a while. This later created a problem: my uncle was accused of sending his son to bring me back from the Islamic school to make me a Christian.

My other uncle noticed that I was not observing the *Salah*, the Muslim prayer. He told me I must not go to my Christian uncle's farm any more. When I did not stop going, he said I had become a *kafiri* (infidel), and if he found me at the farm again he would take measures.

That night the place I stayed in, a mud-brick hut with a thatched roof, was surrounded with people threatening to kill me. So I took my mat and lay down outside, and said anyone who wanted to kill me should come and do so here. I did this to avoid the owner of the hut being hurt. However, no one attacked me.

The following day, I went to my father and told him that since people were already saying I had become a *kafiri*, I wanted to be a Christian. He was quiet for a moment and then asked me if I wanted to destroy their lives and cause them to lose their property, lands and farmlands, and be totally ostracized from the community, and eventually be killed.

As we were talking, my mother came. I did not want her to hear, but she did and began to shout, saying anyone who desired to be Christian in this community would have his hands amputated or be killed. They advised me to continue as a Muslim if I cherished my life. I told them I had made up my mind, and I left them. They collected all my property and threw it out, and said I was cursed and an outcast of the family.

Early in the morning, I was taken to the deputy village head and the local Islamic police. They reported that my uncle deceived me, to convert me to Jesus. I said that that was not true. They sent for more police to question and frighten me. They said if I did not return to Islam then I would be taken to see the district head, and killed by hanging or the electric chair. They said I should realize that I had lost any inheritance in my father's family or the Muslim *ummah* (community).

I continued living in the village. Sometimes they would give me poisoned food and I would eat it without harm. They also made plans to kill me in the night, but God always protected me. This lasted for a year. One day they began to beat me with a rubber whip. I managed to escape and ran into a police station. There they continued to beat me and I almost lost consciousness. They took me from police custody to the *limani* (Muslim cleric).

They planned to kill me, but God did not allow that to happen. I pretended I was going to do what they wanted, and later I went out with one of my guards into the town. When he went into a maize farm to pick some corn I ran away, without money or proper clothes. A Christian organization took me in. The Lord had shown me that he wanted me to attend a Bible college, and after some time, I was brought to the college. There is still a case against me in the *Sharia* law courts in my home town.

Conclusion

It is clear from all these stories that when God changes the heart, persecution cannot persuade converts to forsake him. The courage demonstrated by these new Christians, many of whom come from isolated and staunchly Muslim communities, is a hope and an inspiration.

9.

On the Front Line

The Bible college is based in a large city in northern Nigeria because of the city's proximity to major Islamic centres. Until recent years it had seen less killing of Christians than regions nearby. The founding team believed it would be a safe hub to train those God calls from surrounding regions and nations to spread the gospel far and wide. However, as it is a centre of gospel outreach to the north, the Islamic community is also aware of its strategic importance.

Over the last thirty years, this wider region has seen many attacks against church buildings, Christians, pastors, and their homes and property. Thousands have been killed for their faith. These attacks are in addition to the daily persecution, discrimination and 'honour killings' suffered by those who convert from Islam to Christianity. The persecution against the church in Europe in its early years, prior to Constantine, is mirrored in modern times.

It is hard to understand this from a Western background. On the one hand it is expected that Christians should turn the other cheek, rather than defend themselves; however, many Christians in the West expect their national armies to protect not only their lives, but also their interests at home and abroad. Christians in northern Nigeria often do not have this form of security. Armies may be absent or delayed for days while attacks on Christians continue unabated. What do you do when a group of 100 thugs are coming to kill your family, armed with guns, large knives and petrol bombs? Surely you defend your wife and children? What do you do when these attacks recur every few years, and members of your extended family are brutally murdered? How long can someone endure this?

There are those who, after experiencing attacks over many years, have defended themselves, or have gone out to fight against aggressors. This is not college policy, but it is difficult to judge those who do so. Revenge killings are also often undertaken by people of ethnic groups culturally identified as 'Christians'. They may take 'defence' to another level; when they are repeatedly attacked over the years, they take action. This is essentially a response to an aggression that is *jihadist* in its origin.

However, this is something the international press usually fails to recognize or admit. They may cite 'Christian aggression', but do not explain the causes of it. They may claim the violence and disputes are about land or politics rather than religion, when ultimately it is the *jihadist* issue that lies at the root of it. *Jihadists* enforce Islamic governance in an area whenever they feel they have the numbers to do so.

Troubles in our state escalated after the return to democracy over a decade ago. A Christian governor was elected by the majority of the native peoples of the state. The immigrant Muslim population, along with Muslims nationwide, planned an attack to regain dominance. Truckloads of guns were brought in, sponsored by foreign nations. An attack broke out two days before 9/11

(New York, 2001). The stated aim of this attack was to kill or drive out every Christian from the city. The attacks went on for a couple of weeks, and many people died.

There were more attacks on churches in 2004, and people questioned the team's decision to base the college in a city where violence was ongoing. Our response was that throughout the north there are repeated attacks in every place. This city previously suffered less than others, as the majority of the people, indigenous to the area, identify themselves as ethnic Christian, not Muslim. While we are not reckless, we cannot run away, leaving our friends and students in danger and unsupported.

The city was peaceful when the college was founded in 2007, and remained so until attacks against churches broke out once again in November 2008, continuing for about a week. These were located in a different part of the city so they did not directly affect the college, but rumours of impending escalation kept everybody very cautious. Then relatively free and fair local council election results went against the Islamic politicians. They decided to protest by killing pastors and Christians and burning churches, homes and belongings. Another round of terrorist tactics held the city to ransom again.

The college and students were kept safe, and a general curfew was enforced. More military checkpoints were established, carefully inspecting all goods entering the city, especially bulky food sacks, to stop the import of guns and machetes. Food became scarce and prices escalated. However, we had just bought a large stock of food and supplies, and so were provided for until the attacks subsided and the curfew was lifted.

The lessons of history

History has lessons here for a global perspective, as many around the world are facing similar situations. In our city, the local population has allowed other groups to immigrate into the area over the past century. These people have settled and run businesses peacefully, and the city has become known for its hospitality. It is a desirable place to live, with a fine climate, beautiful surroundings and friendly residents.

The Islamic people groups were among those who have settled here. They bought land and traded with the local populations, which helped the local economy. But it is when these groups feel that they have enough numbers to dominate that they begin the second phase: to gain control of the region.

The local populations are led to believe that they can live together without religious conflict. They benefit from immigration as the economy receives injections of money, and so they turn a blind eye to the possibility of future threats. But when the Islamic groups initiate the second phase, to gain political control by violence, the locals pay the price. The first generation of locals enjoys the economic stimulus, while the next generation pays for it. Propaganda meanwhile obscures this process.

The expressed aim of many devout Muslims is to implement *Sharia* law, which limits freedom of religion and human rights. It is a totalitarian legal system, where every religion other than Islam is unlawful or merely tolerated, while its adherents are subjected to humiliation, financial penalty and social hardship. There are various degrees of intolerance at different times and in different locations. It is also important to see the other side of the issue: Western policies and actions in Islamic regions have not been blameless, but have often caused genuine grievances among Islamic peoples.

Ultimately, it is not about who is right and who is wrong at a national, political, or cultural level. There is just as much corruption in Western politics and business, and even in some churches, but we are often blind to it. There is no truth in the idea that some people, nations or cultures are intrinsically better or more justified. The only redeeming feature is redemption itself: the gospel is the only truth that stands in the final analysis. The Redeemer is all we have to rely on. The gospel is about setting free all those who suffer; whether under the bondage of Islam or under the bondage of Western hedonism. Freedom is in Christ and nowhere else.

10.

Escalation

We had become used to infrequent violence, but were taken by surprise when attacks suddenly broke out again in January 2010 with no obvious trigger. However, we assumed that they would be over in a day or two and would not spread to our part of the city.

The violence started with an attack on several congregations during their Sunday services. In one location, a large Muslim mob went to a small building site next to a church, pretending to be builders. They carried guns and other weapons, and launched the attack from the building site. The international press accepted this charade about the building site, claiming that Christians in the neighbouring church had disrupted builders at work.

Men, women and children were innocent victims of unprovoked aggression. More attacks were planned, and two days later violence broke out in different parts of the city. A number of the aggressors had machine-guns, some of which were mounted on tripods, to pick off people trying to flee, while others went from house to house, dragging people out into the street and slaughtering them. Even previously friendly Muslim neighbours murdered their Christian friends. Corpses that had been hacked to pieces or burnt were left to rot in gutters and drains without pity or mercy.

Over the months and weeks before the attacks, guns had been smuggled into the city, hidden in sacks of rice. The Christians had no guns. In several parts of the city they fled to nearby rocky outcrops to gain a better view of the approaching mob. Muslims gathered on other hill-tops, shouting '*Allahu akbar*' (God is great) and the Christians answered with a loud 'Hallelujah!' in stand-offs reminiscent of the Israelites and the Philistines.

In one battle, described by a participant, Muslims fired on an encampment of Christians. These 'Christians' were a mixture of believers and people of non-Islamic back-ground. The police shot blanks into the air to draw the fire. When the Muslims' bullets had been used up, the police stood aside and allowed the 'Christians' to run into the Islamic battle line with their knives and sticks. They routed the Muslim attackers, and chased them out of the area.

The unprecedented feature of the 2010 attacks is that they came into our part of the city, right where the col-lege is. Here, the attacks were strongest. Hundreds of buildings – houses, shops and churches on or near our road, and at the market-place about half a kilometre from the college – were destroyed and burnt. Many peo-ple were killed, both Christians and Muslims.

The college was on its Christmas break, so only a few students were on the campus. All of the staff and their families were there, but the dangerous conditions of that time meant that every other family living on the estate had fled, leaving all of their property behind. It was an ideal opportunity for violent looters.

The college campus was rented from a Muslim, an elder among the Islamic community and one of the instigators of the 2001 attacks – although he now claims to be a reformed, moderate Muslim. We associate with moderate

Muslims, and do business together in normal daily affairs. The Muslim community approached our landlord, asking him to evict us from the estate because we are a Christian organization that trains pastors who are converting Muslims to Christ and planting churches in Islamic areas. He refused to comply, saying we were godly people and he had no cause to disturb us.

It is astounding how the Lord arranges things for our good. Occupying a Muslim's estate meant that we were not attacked by Muslims. They would not burn down a large Muslim estate, or destroy the property of a fellow Muslim. Ironically, in this 2010 attack, it was the so-called 'Christians' who were our main threat. 'Christian' vigilantes went on the rampage to rid the neighbour-hood of the Islamic population, to avenge and prevent further attacks against their families and livelihoods.

Killings, burnings and lootings were carried out in our district over a period of a couple of weeks, during which time a gang of thugs came to the college campus several times to burn it down. They claimed that our landlord was a main organizer of the riots against Christians, and that they would not allow his buildings to remain. Our staff refused to vacate the premises, telling the youths that the campus was being used for the gospel. The thugs returned several times, telling the staff to move all their property out so that the mob could set the buildings on fire. The staff continued to persuade them not to do so, and refused to leave. The mob, armed with crude weapons, destroyed the compound outer wall and one of the unoccupied buildings on the estate, and then final-ly left. The property – not just that of the landlord, but everything inside the houses belonging to the tenants who had fled – was thus kept safe.

We could not put the college property on trucks and move it to a safer place, because travelling was too dangerous. However, we did move the wives and children off the campus, and the staff mounted a twenty-four hour security surveillance, assisted by local armed policemen who we were able to employ for this task.

The college leader lives a short distance from the campus. The house next door was burnt down, while he and his family had locked themselves up inside their house, which was left unharmed. All he could do was to communicate with the staff at the college by phone, while it still retained enough charge. There was no electricity in the city and he could not use the diesel generator, as the noise of the motor would have attracted attention.

We tried to make plans to protect the staff in the future, and did consider owning a gun, with proper official training and licensing. However, we decided against it, as this was no guarantee of safety. Indeed, a gun might only serve to attract a larger force of attackers.

During this time, there were reports of soldiers entering houses and shooting people. Some soldiers were gunning down victims on the streets. It was then discovered that Islamists were wearing fake military uniforms, pretending to be soldiers so that they could more easily gain the trust of others and kill them. One of the tailors responsible for making the uniforms was subsequently caught and prosecuted, but he received only a three-month sentence, despite the carnage he had been party to. With such leniency imposed on the court system by groups associated with the UN, it is not surprising that the police want to deal with issues 'on the street', since they are the ones whose lives are first at risk. This is why some criminals were reported to have been 'shot while escaping'!

In another place, Muslims took the bodies of dead Christians and laid them on the floor of their mosque, then brought in the press, claiming they were Muslims whom Christians had killed. The international press did not know the truth, and reported it the way the Muslims had intended. Similar false reports are widespread, and are deliberately intended to hide the truth from foreigners. Winning the propaganda war is an important part of the long-term Islamic goals.

The demands of love

Distrust makes it even more difficult for genuine Muslim converts. Some have claimed to convert, and then taken the opportunity to burn churches and kill Christians. At times, Muslim spies infiltrate churches and report back to their people, and this makes Christians vulnerable. During the 2010 attacks, a young Muslim carpenter was working at the college. He had been with us for six months, so we had no reason to believe that he would betray us, and he did not. He continued working faithfully, and is friends with one of the team's sons. Every day we pray to remain open to the Lord in these decisions. A lot of the violence occurs because people hear rumours and are motivated by fear and panic. They kill because they are afraid that they themselves will be killed.

A Muslim mechanic has a workshop next to the college, and during the attacks he was wounded and came to us for first aid. The staff treated his wounds and helped him get medical care. A Muslim lady who had lost her home in the attacks came to us each evening for shelter and protection. Christians need to find a way of expressing love during times of difficulty, which is hard to do when they are fearful.

The college staff team has come through situations like this many times over the years. There have been years of near-anarchy and the threat of civil war. We cannot act irresponsibly or presumptuously where the lives of those we work with are at stake, but on the other hand we do not want to shut down the ministry due to fear. Proverbs 28:1 says, 'The wicked flee when no one pursues' (NKJV). There is a place in Christ where love demands that we stand boldly and fearlessly to reach others with the gospel. The purpose of attacks and rumours is to intimidate Christians so they will flee, thus giving up the land, and more importantly, giving up reaching the people with the gospel. And so we are determined to stand firm.

11.

Massacre

Two weeks after the January 2010 attacks, it looked as though the violence had ceased for the time being. The team decided to start lectures again, and students were about to arrive for a new semester. We did not know whether anyone would come, given the conditions, but in fact we had the largest intake of students in the college's short three-year history. The college grew to over two hundred students during those near wartime conditions.

I began to lecture with the other staff. The streets were quiet, as there was still a lot of tension in the city and many people were staying inside. Under a strict dusk-to-dawn curfew, children's schools did not open, as there were too many rumours of impending attacks. Slowly, more pastors came to visit the college, talking about what they had witnessed during the main attacks. Another guest flew in from the UK to lecture for a few weeks. Things looked settled by the time he left.

Some of the team were at the local radio station in March, for a live one-hour gospel programme that airs all through the *Sharia* law states. (We often broadcast these programmes in Hausa, so all the Muslims can hear the gospel.) At the close of the programme we heard the first news of what had happened that morning. Muslim Fulani cattle herdsmen had attacked three villages at 1.30 a.m., when all of the villagers were asleep. An estimated 500 men, women and children had been mercilessly slaughtered with guns and machetes. People were hacked and burned, even pregnant women and babies, with a barbarity to rival that of the Assyrians of old. The villages were very close to the college.

The news deeply shocked the whole population, who could not comprehend the *jihadists'* inhumanity in carrying out such an appalling act. Such brutality had never before been witnessed or even imagined by the native people of the land. Shockwaves radiated internationally. When they looked at row upon row of tiny, mutilated and charred corpses laid out for burial, even foreign news agencies doubted claims that this was an act of retaliation. The Christian governor immediately appealed for forgiveness rather than vengeance. There was no vengeance, but more Christians would be killed before the attacks were over.

In the days following the massacre, rumours began to spread of more Muslims coming into the city to ethnically cleanse the region so they could regain governance of the state. Christians who had begun to come back into the city after the last attack fled once again. Many moved out of the city permanently.

It seemed that people were spying on our homes, and no one knew what was going to happen next. Attacks could spread from the nearby villages to our street; each night could be our last. When we drove to the college each day, the streets were almost empty except for the military. Very few people dared to leave their houses.

However, classes at the college continued, and the students asked us what we thought was going to happen. I believed all would be well, but I said nothing because I felt each person had to pray and gain their own assurance from God. As staff we were careful not to tell people what to do – they had to make their own decisions.

Ngozi, one of the staff, rented a room in a house nearby which was owned by a family from the south of the country. That week she saw a bleeding, wounded Muslim man run through her backyard being pursued by a mob. She heard later that the mob had caught up with him on the street and killed him, afraid he had been sent to gather information to plan the next massacre. She was left in the house on her own, as her landlord and his family fled to the south. Her own family contacted her, pleading with her to leave the city, offering to send her the flight money. She replied that her calling was to stay and teach, and that she was happy to do so.

All the other staff and students said the same, despite their families pleading with them to leave. Each one was free to do what they believed was right. One staff member said to his family: 'I am staying. We know this work is of the Lord, and we will not walk away from it. This is the most fulfilling thing I have ever been involved in.' They answered, 'At least send your wife away,' but she replied, 'My place is to stay here with my husband.'

The students stayed on alert throughout the night because of rumours about truckloads of Muslims approaching. Sarah lived in rented accommodation next to the campus. She was sitting with her flatmate, who wasn't a student, when a stray bullet passed through their window and hit the other woman, wounding her.

Large groups held demonstrations in the city, claiming that the army should have prevented the village massacres. Some of these demonstrations were close to the college, and there was no telling what violence could develop. The police caught some Muslims while they were making bombs, and one Muslim was killed when a bomb went off.

We constantly and prayerfully considered the situation, as we could not presume to decide the lives of the students, staff and their families. Should we temporarily close? Should we relocate to another city?

College leader Abubakar summed it up: 'There is no safer city in the Islamic areas. If we moved south, out of the Islamic region, we would no longer reach Muslims with the gospel. Besides, there are other dangers there – armed robbery, kidnapping – so the safest place to be is in the will of God.' Two junior staff members overheard some of this. 'If you close the college we will make placards and march in the street in protest!' they joked.

The students asked us to teach them what to do in a crisis. 'Go to work in the morning and come home at night,' we responded. The staff generally work twelve hours or more a day, often seven days a week. Their love and faith are inspiring.

'What did the early church do under persecution?' the students asked. Looking in the book of Acts, we found that at first, many died. This went on for about 300 years until Christianity became more dominant. The disciples were not afraid when persecuted. They asked God to give them boldness to preach the gospel: the early church overcame the enemy by converting them, eventually winning them to Christ. The Bible teaches us that we should preach the gospel to all people, including the enemy; we should continue to love the enemy (see Matt. 5:44).

I told the students the story of a pastor who had emigrated to a safer and more prosperous nation. He prayed, 'Lord, thank you for taking me to this safe and peaceful city to live . . .' but he fell asleep in the middle of his prayer. Then I told them that years ago someone in the West said to me, 'We are praying for you, in the jungles of Africa with the witchdoctors!' and that I answered, 'The pew you sit on every week is more dangerous. You can fall asleep spiritually sitting on that pew and miss the purpose of God!'

The students were encouraged by these illustrations. The week passed; confidence and boldness began to return to the student body. Things began to settle down in the city again, even though sporadic attacks on a smaller scale continued.

And today?

It is likely that these conditions will persist for the short and medium term – after all, this is the front line. The gospel is pushing north, and many Muslims are being saved. The oppressors are not going to let this happen without a fight, but we are confident that the gospel will prevail. We know that we cannot back down, because our commission is to preach. The early disciples did not retreat, so why should we? We must grasp every opportunity to reach out and help people in need, including Muslims.

The attacks are less widespread, but they do continue. A mob entered a pastor's house on a Saturday morning and murdered his wife and children. Others were killed that same day, and churches burnt. Another man was killed across the road from the college. On Christmas Eve 2010, churches in our city were bombed during their services, and many Christians were killed. We are no better than any who have laid down their lives for the gospel, but we are grateful for the miracle that none of our people in the college or mission stations have been hurt. Even the car owned by one of our staff, which was parked at a mechanic's workshop during some attacks, was the only vehicle there not set ablaze.

Despite the city currently being the most dangerous in the nation, we are constantly contacted by brave souls with a sincere desire to serve. Osagie, who graduated some years ago, emailed us saying that the Lord had told him to travel north and work with us. A few weeks later he appeared with his wife and child, having resigned from his church. Our ministry board decided he should pastor in one of our churches in the city, and the family is doing very well. Recently we received a note from Emeka, one of our former students, who went on to a foreign university: 'I have heard much about your work. I am thrilled by your sacrifice and the growth of the kingdom. If you need my service, I am willing to come.'

Constant vigilance is required. Newspapers recently reported a large cargo of guns, munitions, rocket launchers and grenades found during an attempt to smuggle them into the region. Admitting these were brought in by Muslims, the international press falsely claimed Christians in the region also have military capacity. It must be noted that there is no evidence in support of this claim, nor is there any report of true Christians initiating armed attacks or fighting back with sophisticated weapons of any type. They may defend themselves, but only do so when attacked.

The federal government is responsible for, and in control of, the security forces. For the most part, there is discipline and the forces are fairly well supplied. The state government is also vigilant in very difficult circumstances. Paul's instruction to Timothy – that we pray for those in authority over us (see 1 Tim. 2:1–4) so that we may live in peace to spread the gospel – becomes more urgent in these times. Government is God's gift to the people. There are courageous, strong and righteous

Christians among the leaders of the nation. This is another reason that we do not run. They need our support.

12.

On the Move in the Middle East

From our earliest days in Africa, Beth and I had a desire to train pastors for the Middle East, and Alexandria seemed to be an appropriate place to do this. Finding a central hub and training the local people is the best way of getting the gospel moving throughout a region. Paul taught at Ephesus for two years in the school of Tyrannus, and the word of God went from there throughout the entire province then called Asia.

God's love for the Arabs is shown by the story of Ishmael in Genesis, whom Abraham drove away with Hagar (see Gen. 21:8–21). To provide for their needs, God showed Hagar a well of water (v. 19). The living water is Jesus. Many Muslims, spiritual descendents from the Arabic, Ishmaelite culture, are coming to know Jesus, drawing on living water from the well of life. Globally, there is a growing fear of Islam, but we believe that God is opening up Islamic nations for the gospel, and that we should be involved in it ourselves. Large numbers of churches are opening throughout the Middle East.

After prayer in 2009, the team felt it was time to go to Egypt. Although we had a few contacts, these did not seem the place to start, and no door seemed to open for us.

We decided that one of the team should go and investigate the possibilities, and John was chosen for the task.

John's story

John grew up in a religious Christian family in a northern Islamic area. His mother was a churchgoer, and he occasionally – and reluctantly – went too, but was far more interested in causing trouble, until the day he was invited to a Christian students' meeting at his new school. He went along, curious to know why so many attended and were so excited about everything. He was impressed with the enthusiasm of the preacher, but did not really take much notice of what was being said. However, when the preacher started praying for the sick, and people were healed before John's eyes, he started paying attention! He began to recall what the preacher had said. He could not remember the details but knew that he was thoroughly ashamed to be there, that he was evil, hopelessly lost in sin, and had no right to see the power of God revealed through these miracles. He had missed the altar call, but knew his only hope was to beg Jesus for mercy, which he did, there on his seat, and was totally transformed, beginning a new journey of faith that day. Ever since then, John has been characterized by boldness and enthusiasm, a passionate evangelist, always ready for a new challenge.

Over the years John has planted several churches, but he had never been out of the country before. Nevertheless, his ticket and visa to Egypt were arranged. We prayed together, 'Lord, we are going to a new region, a new culture, and to the Eastern Church where we have never been before. We do not know anyone, and we do not want to presume about what you want us to do. Help us. Do what you want and lead us.'

Experience in the north of our nation, reaching out to Muslims and non-Westerners, has taught us to be careful not to mix politics with the gospel. We have been on platforms in the north where national flags are arranged behind the pulpit; especially American, Australian, British and Israeli flags. But we should not present the gospel to Muslims, Hausa, Arabs, Persians or Turks in this way. It is an alliance of the gospel with nationalism that is not appropriate. Jesus did not do this. We are ambassadors of Christ's kingdom, not of a nation state.

We also did not want to go to the Middle East insisting upon theologies that have developed in some sectors of Western church history. It is not appropriate to go into Egypt, which has had the gospel since the apostle Paul's day, and say, 'We are the missionaries, so let us show you a more excellent way.' We want to preach only the lordship of Jesus Christ, and act as helpers to the ministries which already exist there.

So in June 2009, John set off for Egypt with one phone number for a contact in Alexandria he had not been introduced to. The contact – a pastor – did not know John, or even that John was coming. Arriving at the hotel in Cairo he called the number, and the next morning travelled to Alexandria and introduced himself to the pastor. Because of Christian persecution in Egypt, John was not sure if he would be welcomed. What happened next took us all by surprise.

The pastor hired a flat for John and arranged meetings for him all over Egypt. He began preaching in Coptic, Baptist, Methodist, Presbyterian, Anglican and Pentecostal churches, and at Cairo University. He preached every day for a month, and reached thousands of people with the gospel. Muslims were saved, a deaf boy was healed, as was a lady blind in one eye; others spoke in tongues (see 1 Cor. 12) or had demons cast out of them.

These miracles frequently caused quite a stir. People started coming from different cities, meeting John on the street on his way to and from meetings, asking for prayer. Prayer on the streets, other than Muslim prayer, is illegal in Egypt, so nearby homes had to be quickly located where house meetings would immediately start. There, John would begin preaching and praying for the people. Churches announced five-day revival meetings they hadn't previously planned. Pastors came to meet John and asked him to address their congregations in spontaneous gatherings.

He met wonderful people that the Lord is using in the Middle East. Some Egyptian missionaries were working in the Sudan, preaching and helping believers build worship centres. John met with a lady who had returned from Sudan, and was recovering from several gunshot wounds in her legs. A partner who was with her when they were attacked had been killed, yet she expressed love for the Lord and for the Sudanese and said she wanted to return as soon as she was able. John also met a woman who preaches throughout Syria and invited the college to do outreach there. He preached alongside another Egyptian woman who leads a national ministry reaching thousands in Egypt with the gospel. Anglican theologians are also making an impact there, training leaders to spread the gospel in that nation. An old man, who was an interpreter for American Pentecostal evangelist T.L. Osborn when he preached in the region years ago, met with John. These and other examples demonstrated what the Lord was (and is) doing through an active church suffering much persecution.

While there, John was introduced to a Spirit-filled Anglican theologian who has since translated *Christ in You*, a book published by the college, into Arabic. John also made plans for a pastors' conference in Egypt in

2010. We hoped that this conference would bring together people from throughout the Middle East, so it was
with a great sense of excitement that we prepared for it.

Before the conference I contacted Brother Andrew's
ministry, Open Doors. I just wanted to speak to someone
who had more experience in the Middle East, after reading his book *Light Force* (written with Al Janssen, Grand
Rapids, MI: Revell, 2004) which told of many years of
serving the church in Middle Eastern nations. It con-
firmed my belief that God only opens doors for the
gospel and love of Jesus, and not for a mixed gospel/
political message. Brother Andrew phoned me and
shared his knowledge of the situation in the region. It
was a blessing to have this encouragement from him, as
the whole team has admired his work over many years.

About 150 pastors attended the one-week conference,
camping in rooms at the centre where the event was
held. Many of those who attended were pastors of
churches, Egyptian missionaries to nearby Middle
Eastern nations, or evangelists within Egypt. They came
from a range of denominations, and it was tremendous
to hear their stories of faith and loving gospel outreach,
in the face of great persecution – indeed, we heard of
many who had lost their limbs, or their lives, for the sake
of the gospel message. As members of the same family in
Jesus, we felt privileged to be working alongside them.

We met and prayed with a Coptic bishop. The Coptic
people – the indigenous Egyptians – feel that the Arabic
language and Islam have been part of a colonial takeover
since the seventh century. The bishop was banned from seeing us because we were 'evangelicals', so he sneaked
through back alleys to meet us in the home of a Coptic family. The bishop told us a lot about the situation in Egypt,
saying that Cairo, rather than Mecca, was the centre of the
quest for global Islamization. He also told us that more

Muslims in Egypt are turning to Jesus now than at any time in Egypt's history. Most of these are 'underground believers', as in the time of the early church. His words were later echoed by an evangelical leader, who told me that Cairo University is also a hub for fundamentalists, training Islamists and sending them to join professional and political organizations in the West.

We did visit some churches while we were there. Each one had a government armed security guard stationed at the entrance, supposedly 'for the safety of the Christians', but also to monitor what the church was doing. In Egypt it is illegal for Christians to preach outside their church buildings, or to witness to Muslims. The Christians have to be very careful. One of the churches I visited was an old Methodist congregation, where an elderly man stood up with a hymn book to lead the unaccompanied singing. I was surprised and delighted by the spiritual depth of their songs, and thoroughly enjoyed that service. There is no doubt that God is working powerfully in the country, although we can see little above ground of what he is actually doing.

John has since returned from another trip to Egypt where the Lord continued to perform miracles and open doors to new opportunities. At the time of writing, we have planned another conference for Egypt and are expecting 300 pastors, missionaries and evangelists to attend. Many of these are grass roots workers, reaching people with the gospel all over the Middle East in the midst of incredible persecution. We plan to set up a Bible college in Egypt in the coming year, and continue to pray that the Lord will give us a means of maintaining a presence in the nation, supporting pastoral training and being tools for his work. It is God's time for the Middle East.

13.

Impacting Islam

In this book, I have written about Abubakar. He is a founding member of the college, and his father is a Muslim imam (similar in rank to a bishop) and a mechanical engineer. Abubakar grew up in a town with around two hundred and fifty thousand inhabitants, a main centre of education, a strong metal and cement producer, and the largest national producer of cocoa products. Yams, cassava, grain, tobacco and cotton for cloth weaving are grown in abundance among the forests in the rich mountainous soil. Abubakar helped his father, learning mechanics, and also farmed as part of his agricultural science studies.

In the early 1980s he graduated from Islamic school. He had learned to recite much of the Qur'an, spoke and read Arabic, and wanted to become an imam. He planned to further his Islamic studies in Cairo, and perhaps go to the USA to make money before returning home as an Islamic scholar, with a passion to win the world for Islam. He enthusiastically developed his witchcraft powers, as he believed this was the best way to help people who were suffering.

But before Abubakar left for Cairo, the Lord began revealing the gospel to him. First, his cousin invited him to a church service. She told him to respond to the altar call and he did, though he did not really understand it. Later his sister was filled with the Holy Spirit. Abubakar thought she would be afraid to preach the gospel to him, an Islamic student and an occult practitioner, but she claimed the power within her was greater than any power he had known, and that she had no fear.

The Lord used this to get Abubakar's attention. In this world of sickness, death and demonic attack, he desired some way of being able to help those around him. He wanted an ability to influence things for good. Abubakar began to seek this power his sister knew, thinking he would add it to the occult powers he already had.

While at a church service, he was prayed for and was filled with the Holy Spirit. Immediately he began to speak in tongues (see 1 Cor. 12) and this continued for the next thirty-six hours. His life was totally changed. His father disowned him, and tried everything he could to dissuade him from the gospel. Eventually he held a gun to Abubakar's head and threatened to shoot him. Abubakar boldly and calmly refused to recant, and his father backed down.

Destroying all his occult possessions, he grew in his faith. Abubakar began to evangelize, and found the Lord was setting people free from demonic oppression and healing others of sicknesses. He wanted to study theology, and in 1991 he enrolled in the college in the south. It was there that Beth and I met him.

We worked closely together during his student days, and as a student prefect Abubakar helped the growing southern college with total commitment. Seeing his father at his graduation was a surprise, but Abubakar was honoured and delighted. Today they are close again.

After graduating, he stayed on as a member of the staff. I was director of the college, and he worked as my personal assistant, as well as overseeing three churches. When we opened the new college in the north, Abubakar's leadership and development roles blossomed further, as he forged relationships with university professors, government officials and community leaders, and led the entire ministry through much development and many trials.

Years after Abubakar's coming to Christ, many of his family members have now also been saved – when one of his brothers is on holiday from university, he serves the college diligently as a volunteer.

Building for the future

In the years since the college in the north was founded, we had settled into the region, formed relationships with the local community, and opened various arms of gospel outreach. Continually blessed with resources from friends and prayer partners, the college had grown from thirty-three to 200 students. The library held 3,000 quality books and thirty online research computers. A primary school had opened for children of staff and the wider community. New churches and mission stations had started. Seven pastors' conferences had been held in different northern cities. Weekly TV and radio broadcasts had begun, the radio broadcast reaching a potential 80 million people, the majority of whom were in Islamic *Sharia* law centres. *Christ in You*, a major book for the college, had been completed and translated into Arabic and Hausa, and Egypt had opened up to us to develop future pastoral training in the Middle East.

However, we knew that we were building for the future and that others would take on the work after us and continue reaching many with the gospel. For this, we needed land for a permanent site for the college. And so, near the end of 2009, Abubakar and other college leaders went to the head chief in a locality just outside our city, to discuss buying some land. They sat down together in his home, shared gifts and talked. Abubakar explained why they had come to visit him – to buy thirty acres of land in his area. The chief was in favour, and keen to develop the area, and so he spoke to the landowners on our behalf. They wanted a high price, but the chief persuaded them to reduce the amount they were charging. We knew we were getting a good deal, but it was still a lot of money for us – money which we did not have. We told them we would sign for the thirty acres if we could seal the price and pay in five instalments to the five separate families who owned portions of the land. They agreed.

We needed a large amount for the first payment, and a friend contacted us to say he was selling his coin collection in order to help. Another friend in a small country town also contacted us. He had read the theology book the college had published, and said it had helped him a lot, and so he wanted to make a donation towards the work. It was another large gift, and together the two gifts enabled us to make the first payment.

The second payment was the largest one. We prayed about it. Our family was now based in the UK so that our children could complete their education. Beth spent most of her time there while I 'commuted' to the college, staying for a while each time.

Eleven years before, a friend had contacted us and said that since we needed a base in the UK, he wanted to help us to buy a house so that we would not be wasting our money on rent. He provided the funds for a deposit and for the stamp duty. Thank God for people who do not live life for themselves, but to be a blessing to God's work! A friend in the UK took us to a bank to ask for a loan. 'Do you have a national insurance number, a salaried job, or a fixed income?' they asked. 'No, no, and no,' were our answers. They gave us the loan, which totally surprised our friend! Eleven years later we had some equity in the house, and we thought about using it to take a loan for the second payment on the land for the Bible college. The recent recession meant UK banks often refused to make loans. The coalition government has cut down even more on spending, to try to eradicate its deficit. Yet with God's blessing, our credit rating is such that our bank has been contacting us trying to get us to take loans, even in a poor economic climate. Up until this point we had always refused.

As land is a fixed asset for continued gospel ministry, we decided to take out a personal loan to buy the second and third portions of the college's permanent site. We did not know how the fourth and fifth payments would come, but God remains the Great Provider: a friend in the UK gave us enough money in his will to complete the final payments, without our knowing of his plan.

Aiming to grow

The land is on the outskirts of the city, in the direction in which the city is growing. After we signed for it, the governor tarmacked the adjacent road for us. A small river borders the site at one end – providing water that we can use for farm irrigation. We have now had a survey carried out for development, and at time of writing are in the process of preparing it for the next pastors' conference, which is aimed at equipping and encouraging gospel workers in the north.

This will mean building a perimeter security fence with a shelter for the night security guards, sinking a bore hole, erecting large elevated water tanks, putting in a big power generator, building toilet blocks and obtaining enough bedding, chairs and tents to cater for sizeable crowds. These provisions will serve the ministry in the years ahead. We have invited speakers for the conference and have asked mission organizations in the area (such as Wycliffe, CAPRO and several others) to take part.

Brother Andrew of Open Doors described our city and state as being under a siege that was carefully planned and designed by Islamic extremists to bring it into line with *Sharia* law. Sure enough, there have been more attacks against Christians in our city in 2011. Christians were shot at, stabbed, burnt and blown up. Islamists threatened even stronger *jihad* before the 2011 elections. One of our churches was burnt down. No one was hurt but they made death threats against the pastors. However, God even turned this to good; the pastors said they wanted to rebuild, so our supporters gave them the money, and they now have a far better building! We also bought land near that church and plan to build a school there soon.

Another of our churches in a nearby city was burnt down, too. Again, none of the people were hurt, but other Christians in the city were killed. The gospel is growing and spreading fast in these Islamic states, and this persecution is the response to fear of the gospel. We are convinced that soon there will be so many converts to Jesus that the fighting will stop.

Our staff and students prayed and trusted God through all these threats and the college has continued to grow, reaching 250 students this year. We aim to continue to grow until we have 800 students all training to plant churches in the north and Middle East. We don't have the resources for this, but God does. We have peace in the city now, for which we thank God.

Our commission

I have spent part of this year meeting graduates in cities and villages in different parts of the nation, especially in the remote, cut-off but very highly populated areas. There is great revival in all of these places. I have met hundreds of graduates this year alone, all serving the Lord with great blessing on their lives and work. We continue to help where we can, assisting graduates to buy land, build schools, or set up church buildings. We will soon hold a second pastors' conference in Chad, where a former graduate oversees 150 churches in one of the most difficult nations on earth, suffering great poverty and aggressive Islamization.

As the Lord reveals himself to more Hausa and Fulani people, the tide is quickly turning. Our work, and other projects like it, continues to grow, rapidly expanding in student numbers and in the churches and mission fields opening in this and other nations. Just as Jesus said, 'The harvest is plentiful but the workers are few. Ask the Lord of the harvest, therefore, to send out workers into his harvest field' (Matt. 9:37,38, NIV). Jesus trained and sent them out, first twelve, then seventy, then 120, then a great multitude went out from Jerusalem, everywhere, preaching the gospel, and God worked with them.

This nation will continue to blossom as a major gospel force in Africa and globally. As the gospel continues to advance northward in the nations around the Sahara desert, this permanent site will be used to train thousands of church leaders, and to teach vocational skills to people of all backgrounds from the local community and interior regions. Plans are well under way to develop the new land as the permanent base of outreach to the north. Small business centres and agriculture will serve in training people of all backgrounds and subsidize the ongoing missions programme.

We would ask you to become part of the team and of the harvest, whether you join us or support our cause by praying or giving. There are many more stories that have yet to be told, and countless others yet to come to pass. Gospel proclamation is our commission. May we continue to be found faithfully, earnestly, lovingly, enthusiastically, joyfully and boldly preaching the wonderful news of forgiveness, redemption, and empowerment through God's grace!

Contact

If you would like to learn more about or support the work we are doing, please contact us at:

fearless.love.africa@gmail.com

We will ask you for a reference for identification, before establishing personal contact with you. We ask you to join our team in reaching out with the gospel and look forward to hearing from you.

Authentic

We trust you enjoyed reading this book from
Authentic Media Limited. If you want to be informed
of any new titles from this author and other exciting
releases you can sign up to the Authentic Book
Club online:

www.authenticmedia.co.uk/bookclub

Contact us
By Post: Authentic Media Limited
52 Presley Way
Crownhill
Milton Keynes
MK8 0ES

E-mail: info@authenticmedia.co.uk

Follow us: